Overcoming Prejudice

Character Education

Being a Leader and Making Decisions

Being Fair and Honest

Dealing with Bullying

Dealing with Frustration and Anger

Handling Peer Pressure

Handling Teamwork and Respect for Others

Managing Conflict Resolution

Managing Responsibilities

Overcoming Prejudice

Character Education

Overcoming Prejudice

TRACEY BAPTISTE

INTRODUCTION BY CONSULTING EDITORS
Madonna M. Murphy, Ph.D.
University of St. Francis
and **Sharon L. Banas**
former Values Education Coordinator,
Sweet Home Central School District, New York

CHELSEA HOUSE
PUBLISHERS
An imprint of Infobase Publishing

Jackie Robinson of the Brooklyn Dodgers (right) poses with teammates (left to right) Johnny "Spider" Jorgensen, Harold "Pee Wee" Reese, and Eddie Stanky in the dugout during Robinson's first official game on April 15, 1947 in Brooklyn, New York.

Character Education: Overcoming Prejudice
Copyright ©2009 by Infobase Publishing

Chelsea House
An imprint of Infobase Publishing
132 West 31st Street
New York NY 10001

Library of Congress Cataloging-in-Publication Data
Baptiste, Tracey.
  Overcoming prejudice / Tracey Baptiste.
    p. cm. — (Character education)
  Includes bibliographical references and index.
  ISBN 978-1-60413-119-2 (hardcover)
  1. Prejudices—Prevention—Juvenile literature. 2. Toleration—Juvenile literature. I. Title. II. Series.
  HM1091.B36 2009
  303.3'85—dc22   2008025306

Chelsea House books are available at special discounts when purchased in bulk quantities for businesses, associations, institutions, or sales promotions. Please call our Special Sales Department in New York at (212) 967-8800 or (800) 322-8755.

You can find Chelsea House on the World Wide Web at
http://www.chelseahouse.com

Text design by Annie O'Donnell
Cover design by Takeshi Takahashi

Printed in the United States

Bang FOF 10 9 8 7 6 5 4 3 2 1

This book is printed on acid-free paper.

All links and Web addresses were checked and verified to be correct at the time of publication. Because of the dynamic nature of the Web, some addresses and links may have changed since publication and may no longer be valid.

CONTENTS

Introduction   **7**
by **Madonna M. Murphy, Ph.D.**, professor of
education at University of St. Francis, Joliet, Illinois,
and **Sharon L. Banas**, former character education
coordinator and middle school social studies teacher, Sweet
Home School District, Amherst and Tonawanda, New York

1 What Is Prejudice?   **13**

2 Enemies and Allies   **21**

3 Playing to Win   **39**

4 Separate Education   **52**

5 Women and Politics   **68**

6 Coming to America   **83**

7 Image Is Everything   **95**

8 Building Tolerance   **106**

Glossary   **112**

Bibliography   **114**

Further Resources   **117**

Picture Credits   **119**

Index   **120**

About the Author and Consultants   **126**

INTRODUCTION

On February 14, 2008, as these books were being edited, a shooting occurred at Northern Illinois University (NIU) in DeKalb, Illinois. A former NIU graduate student, dressed in black and armed with a shotgun and two handguns, opened fire from the stage of a lecture hall. The shooter killed five students and injured 16 others before committing suicide. What could have led someone to do this? Could it have been prevented?

When the shooting started, student Dan Parmenter and his girlfriend, Lauren Debrauwere, who was sitting next to him, dropped to the floor between the rows of seats. Dan covered Lauren with his body, held her hand, and began praying. The shield of Dan's body saved Lauren life, but Dan was fatally wounded. In that hall, on February 14, 2008—Valentine's Day—one person's deed was horrific and filled with hate; another's was heroic and loving.

The purpose of this series of books is to help prevent the occurrence of this kind of violence by offering readers the character education and social and emotional skills they need to control their emotions and make good moral choices. This series includes books on topics such as coping with bullying, conflicts, peer pressure, prejudice, anger and frustration, and numerous responsibilities, as well as learning how to handle teamwork and respect for others, be fair and honest, and be a good leader and decision-maker.

In his 1992 book, *Why Johnny Can't Tell Right from Wrong*,[1] William Kilpatrick coined the term "moral illiteracy" and dedicated a whole chapter to it. Today, as he points out, people often do not recognize when they are in a situation that calls for a moral choice, and they are not able to define what is right and what is wrong in that situation. The California-based Josephson Institute of Ethics agrees with these concerns. The institute states that we have a "character deficit" in our society today and points out that increasing numbers of young people across the United States—from well-to-do as well as disadvantaged backgrounds—demonstrate reckless disregard for fundamental standards of ethical conduct.

According to the 2006 *Josephson Institute Report Card on the Ethics of American Youth*, our children are at risk. This report sets forth the results of a biannual written survey completed in 2006 by more than 36,000 high school students across the country. The compilers of the report found that 82 percent of the students surveyed admitted that they had lied to a parent about something significant within the previous year. Sixty percent admitted to having cheated during a test at school, and 28 percent admitted to having stolen something from a store.[2] (Various books in this series will tell of other findings in this report.) Clearly, helping young people to develop character is a need of national importance.

The United States Congress agrees. In 1994, in the joint resolution that established National Character Counts Week, Congress declared that "the character of a nation is only as strong as the character of its individual citizens." The resolution also stated that "people do not automatically develop good character and, therefore, conscientious efforts must be made by youth-influencing institutions . . . to help young people develop the essential traits and characteristics that comprise good character."[3]

Many stories can be told of people who have defended our nation with character. One of the editors of this series knew one such young man named Jason Dunham. On April 24, 2004, Corporal Jason L. Dunham was serving with the United States Marines in Iraq. As Corporal Dunham's squad was conducting a reconnaissance mission, the men heard sounds of rocket-propelled grenades and small arms fire. Corporal

Dunham led a team of men toward that fire to assist their battalion commander's ambushed convoy. An insurgent leaped out at Corporal Dunham, and he saw the man release a grenade. Corporal Dunham alerted his team and immediately covered the grenade with his helmet and his body. He lost his own life, but he saved the lives of others on his team.

In January 2007, the Dunham family traveled to Washington, D.C., where President George W. Bush presented them with Corporal Dunham's posthumously awarded Congressional Medal of Honor. In the words of the Medal of Honor citation, "By his undaunted courage, intrepid fighting spirit, and unwavering devotion to duty, Corporal Dunham gallantly gave his life for his country."[4]

Thomas Lickona, the author of several books including *Educating for Character* and *Character Matters*, explains that the premise of character education is that there are objectively good human qualities—virtues—that are enduring moral truths. Courage, fortitude, integrity, caring, citizenship, and trustworthiness are just a few examples. These moral truths transcend religious, cultural, and social differences and help us to distinguish right from wrong. They are rooted in our human nature. They tell us how we should act with other human beings to promote human dignity and build a well-functioning and civil society—a society in which everyone lives by the golden rule.[5]

To develop his or her character, a person must understand core virtues, care about them, and act upon them. This series of books aims to help young readers *want* to become people of character. The books will help young people understand such core ethical values as fairness, honesty, responsibility, respect, tolerance of others, fortitude, self-discipline, teamwork, and leadership. By offering examples of people today and notable figures in history who live and have lived these virtues, these books will inspire young readers to develop these traits in themselves.

Finally, through these books, young readers will see that if they act on these moral truths, they will make good choices.

They will be able to deal with frustration and anger, manage conflict resolution, overcome prejudice, handle peer pressure, and deal with bullying. The result, one hopes, will be middle schools, high schools, and neighborhoods in which young people care about one another and work with their classmates and neighbors to develop team spirit.

Character development is a lifelong task but an exciting challenge. The need for it has been with us since the beginning of civilization. As the ancient Greek philosopher Aristotle explained in his *Nicomachean Ethics*:

> The virtues we get by first exercising them . . . so too we become just by doing just acts, temperate by doing temperate acts, brave by doing brave acts. . . . Hence also it is no easy task to be good . . . to do this to the right person, to the right extent, at the right time, with the right motive, and in the right way, that is not easy; wherefore goodness is both rare and laudable and noble. . . . It makes no small difference, then, whether we form habits of one kind or of another from our very youth; it makes a very great difference, or rather all the difference.[6]

This development of one's character is truly *The Ultimate Gift* that we hope to give to our young people. In the movie version of Jim Stovall's book of the same name, a privileged young man receives a most unexpected inheritance from his grandfather. Instead of the sizeable inheritance of cash that he expects, the young man receives 12 tasks—or "gifts"— designed to challenge him on a journey of self-discovery. The gifts confront him with character choices that force him to decide how one can be truly happy. Is it the possession of money that brings us happiness, or is it what we do with the money that we have? Every one of us has been given gifts. Will we keep our gifts to ourselves, or will we share them with others?

Being a "person of character" can have multiple meanings. Psychologist Steven Pinker asks an interesting question in a

January 13, 2008, *New York Times Magazine* article titled "The Moral Instinct": "Which of the following people would you say is the most admirable: Mother Teresa, Bill Gates or Norman Borlaug?" Pinker goes on to explain that although most people would say that, of course, Mother Teresa is the most admirable—a true person of character who ministered to the poor in Calcutta, was awarded the Noble Peace Prize, and was ranked in an American poll as the most admired person in the twentieth century—each of these three is a morally admirable person.

Pinker points out that Bill Gates made billions through his company Microsoft, but he also has decided to give away billions of dollars to help alleviate human misery in the United States and around the world. His charitable foundation is built on the principles that "All lives—no matter where they are being lived—have equal value" and "To whom much is given, much is expected."

Pinker notes that very few people have heard of Norman Borlaug, an agronomist who has spent his life developing high-yielding varieties of crops for third world countries. He is known as the "Father of the Green Revolution" because he used agricultural science to reduce world hunger and, by doing so, saved more than a billion lives. Borlaug is one of only five people in history to have won the Nobel Peace Prize, the Presidential Medal of Freedom, and the Congressional Gold Medal. He has devoted his long professional life and his scientific expertise to making the world a better place.

All of these people—although very different, from different countries, and with different gifts—are people of character. They are, says Pinker, people with "a sixth sense, the moral sense." It is the sense of trying to do good in whatever situation one finds oneself.[7]

The authors and editors of the series *Character Education* hope that these books will help young readers discover their gifts and develop them, guided by a moral compass. "Do good and avoid evil." "Become all that you can be—a person of character." The books in this series teach these things and more. These books will correlate well with national social studies standards of learning. They will help teachers meet state standards for teaching social and emotional skills, as well as state guidelines for teaching ethics and character education.

Madonna M. Murphy, Ph.D.

Author of *Character Education in America's Blue Ribbon Schools* and professor of education, University of St. Francis, Joliet, Illinois

Sharon L. Banas, M.Ed.

Author of *Caring Messages for the School Year* and former character education coordinator and middle school social studies teacher, Sweet Home Central School District, Amherst and Tonawanda, New York

FOOTNOTES

1. William Kilpatrick. *Why Johnny Can't Tell Right from Wrong*, New York: Simon and Schuster, 1992.
2. Josephson Institute, 2006 *Josephson Institute Report Card on the Ethics of American Youth: Part One – Integrity*. Available online at: http://josephsoninstitute.org/pdf/ReportCard_press-release_2006-1013.pdf.
3. House Joint Resolution 366. May 11, 1994, 103rd Congress. 2d Session.
4. U.S. Army Center of Military History. *The Medal of Honor*. Available online at: www.history.army.mil/moh.html.
5. Thomas Lickona, *Educating for Character: Teaching Respect and Responsibility in the Schools*. New York: Bantam, 1991. Thomas Lickona, *Character Matters: How to Help Our Children Develop Good Judgment, Integrity, and Other Essential Virtues*. New York: Simon and Schuster Touchstone Books, 2004.
6. Richard McKeon, editor, "Nicomachean Ethics." *Basic Works of Aristotle*, Chicago: Random House, Clarendon Press, 1941.
7. Steven Pinker, "The Moral Instinct," *The New York Times*, January 13, 2008. Available online at www.newyorktimes.com.

WHAT IS PREJUDICE?

1

"Never look down on anybody unless you're helping him up."

—*Jesse Jackson (1941–),*
civil rights activist and Baptist minister

In Lois Lowry's young-adult novel, *The Giver*, Lowry shows us a world without color. Everything is black and white. The color red is something shocking. Fortunately, we do not live in a world like that. Every shade of every color explodes around us. Every person has a different face and a different personality that shines. Tolerance means accepting all of these differences. A tolerant person tries to find the good in all people. Tolerance may seem like a simple thing, but prejudice has been a part of the world that we live in for a long time.

Think of your friends. These are probably the people who are most like you. You may like the same kind of music. You may wear similar kinds of clothes. You may all come from the same neighborhood, but you are all still different. You think differently. You have different families. You are tolerant of the differences among your friends because you respect them. In the same way, being tolerant means that you respect everyone and are tolerant of them no matter how different they may seem.

Prejudice means to prejudge something without knowing anything about it. Tolerance means being fair and objective. It also means showing interest in things that are new and different.

DOES PREJUDICE AFFECT ME?

Prejudice has affected every group of people at one time or another. It can take many forms. People can be prejudiced against those of a different race, culture, belief system, gender, appearance, or economic level, or those who have different abilities. In a culture of differences, prejudice can affect any person at any time for any number of reasons. If you live in

MAKING SNAP JUDGMENTS

In journalist Malcolm Gladwell's book, *Blink*, he explores the kind of thinking that happens "in the blink of an eye." He says he believes that in the first two seconds of an activity, such as meeting someone, reading a book, or looking at a product we want to buy, our minds jump to a series of conclusions. Gladwell believes that these conclusions are both powerful and important. In some cases, these conclusions can be bad, but in others, they can be good. This kind of decision-making is called rapid cognition. It influences everything from profiling tactics used by police officers to criteria used by people figuring out whom they want to date.

Gladwell says he got the idea for the book a few years ago when he decided to grow his—usually very short—hair long. He says that he started getting stopped for speeding tickets and that on one occasion he was nearly arrested for resembling a police sketch of a criminal. Gladwell pointed out to the officers that he was shorter, weighed less, and had no facial features in common with the sketch. The only thing they had in common was a head of long, curly hair. It got him to thinking about the kinds of snap judgments people make and, more importantly, why people make them.

a community of people who have any kinds of these differences, then prejudice affects you.

You may have already experienced prejudice in your life. Have you ever seen or heard someone being made fun of because they look or act differently? Have you ever heard jokes targeted at a certain group of people? Have you ever experienced someone being excluded from an activity because of what they believe or what they look like? Have you ever witnessed others laughing at someone's disability, gossiping, and name-calling? All of these are examples of prejudice.

You may think, "I am not doing these things. Prejudice has nothing to do with me." But a tolerant person does not allow

The Implicit Association Test uses the same theory of rapid cognition to uncover people's hidden biases. The test can be found at https://implicit.harvard.edu/implicit/. Visitors to the Web site can participate in research or take demonstration tests. The demonstration tests use images and words to look at people's preferences in a number of categories.

There are race tests that explore people's implicit preferences for one race over another. Included are Asian/white, black/white, Native American/white, and Arab-Muslim/other nationalities and religions. One of the tests even explores the idea of lighter versus darker skin tones.

Two of the tests explore gender biases. The Gender-Career test explores the link between women/family and men/careers. The Gender-Science test finds a slight link between liberal arts and females, and science and males. Other tests explore people's preferences regarding weight (fat/thin), age (young/old), and disability (abled/disabled). One other test rates people's ability to recognize the religious symbols of numerous world religions.

these kinds of things to happen while they are around. A tolerant person will show respect for the people being shown prejudice. He or she will say, "You should not say those things" or "That isn't right," or he or she may try to befriend the person being shown prejudice. It may be easier to keep your head down and ignore what others are doing, but what people say and how people react still affects the person being shown intolerance.

Think of Eric Harris and Dylan Klebold, who in 1999 killed a teacher and 12 students and injured several others at their high school in Jefferson County, Colorado. The two teens set off bombs in the school, opened fire on their classmates, and later committed suicide. Many believe that their actions were caused by the facts that they felt discriminated against because of how much money their families had and they were bullied by the school athletes. It was also suggested that other influences included their use of violent movies and video games, as well as prescription anti-depressants by one of the shooters. Harris and Klebold's actions were extreme and heartbreaking to many people that had never acted against them, and what they did affected the entire community. If even one person in the community you live in feels the negative effect of discrimination in his or her life, then your community is affected, too. You are a part of your community. Saying or doing something to help others makes their lives easier and also makes the community a better one in which to live.

Words and actions are not the only things that can hurt. Certain symbols and images have significance to groups of people. The swastika is one of the most powerful of these negative images. The swastika is a 3,000-year-old symbol that has appeared in the cultures of Native American, European, Asian, and African peoples. The word *swastika* comes from a language called Sanskrit. Its original meaning was "good-luck charm." When the German Third Reich began to use the symbol on its flag, the swastika's meaning turned negative. The Third Reich, under Hitler, persecuted

Protestors marched to Jena High School in Jena, La., on Martin Luther King Jr. Day in 2008. Their peaceful protest was in opposition to the arrest of six black students who were arrested for allegedly beating a white classmate two years earlier. Considering the details of the incident, protestors felt the students—dubbed the "Jena Six"—were punished too harshly.

and murdered nearly 6 million people. Most of them were of Jewish faith. The swastika became a symbol of hatred toward Jews.

A noose is a symbol of death, but a noose hanging from a tree means something even more offensive to African Americans. On August 31, 2006, a black student asked the principal of Jena High School in Jena, Louisiana, if he could sit under a certain tree in the school's courtyard. The tree had been viewed by some as "the white tree," where the mostly white school population sat. The principal informed the student he

(continues on page 20)

TWO SIDES TO A STORY

David Lazerson calls himself an "awakener," not a teacher. Yet, education has been his passion for most of his life. After becoming a rabbi in 1975, Dr. Laz, as he calls himself, turned his passion for religion to a passion for students with special needs. In 1981, he won the New York State Teacher of the Year Award for his techniques in teaching students with special needs. Dr. Laz is always looking for a way to reach his students and inspire them, and he allows himself to be inspired by them as well.

In 1999, he published the book, *Skullcaps 'n' Switchblades,* a first-hand account of his experience teaching learning-disabled kids in an inner-city school in Buffalo, New York. Later that same year, seven-year-old Gavin Cato was struck by a car carrying a Hasidic Jewish leader in the Crown Heights community in Brooklyn, New York. A private ambulance arrived to assist the driver but left the injured child, who was later transported to a hospital by a public ambulance. Cato later died, and the incident sparked race riots in the community.

Community leaders turned to Dr. Laz for help. Along with Reverend Paul Chandler, a black youth minister, the two assembled a meeting at P.S. 167, a Brooklyn middle school. They wanted to talk to the youths of the community and try to stem the ongoing violence. The meeting was tense at first, with the two groups on separate sides of the room. Then they began asking each other questions about their style of clothing and the way they wore their hair. It was clear to Dr. Laz and Reverend Chandler that even though the two groups had lived in the same neighborhood for 20 years, they knew nothing about each other. However, they were glad that the kids were asking questions about each other, rather than commenting on stereotypes, which are general images that people attribute to groups.

According to a 2002 report in the New York newspaper *The Village Voice,* the meeting produced the slogan "Increase the Peace" and a band called The CURE. *CURE* stands for Communication, Understanding, Respect, and Education. The band is made up of Dr. Laz, Reverend Chan-

The band The CURE travels throughout the United States spreading a message of mutual respect and increasing the peace. Band members include *(left to right)* Didier (sax), Dr. Laz (guitar and vocals), James (drums), and Reverend Paul Chandler (vocals and percussion).

dler, and youths from the Hasidic and black Crown Heights communities. Their blend of Jewish music and rap is an unexpected combination.

There is a quote from Mario Cuomo, the former governor of New York State, on Dr. Laz's Web site. It says, "Dr. Laz has helped people establish friendships across racial and religious lines, stressing common values that unite us all and emphasizing that diversity is a strength rather than a weakness." Many others have recognized Dr. Laz and The CURE for their promotion of tolerance. Project CURE has won numerous civic awards, including the Mother Hale Award, the Dr. Martin Luther King Jr. "Fulfilling the Dream" Award, the New York Foundation Peace Award, and the John Lindsay Award. On Dr. Laz's Web site, he says, "We've come a long ways, but there's still lots to be done." He also believes "we're all connected."

(continued from page 17)

could sit wherever he liked. The next morning, nooses were hanging from the tree. Some people viewed the nooses as a threat. It reminded them of a time when black men and women were killed by lynch mobs in retaliation for real or imagined offenses. They felt that the nooses were symbols of anti-black feelings. Others felt that the act was just a prank. Either way, the image of nooses hanging from a tree was hurtful to many people.

Many other symbols and images cause hurt for those who see them. Some people feel that symbols of hate can be more painful than unkind words or even physical violence because they affect an entire community, not just the person or people at which the image is directed.

ENEMIES AND ALLIES

2

"People fear what they do not understand."
—Bruce Lee (1940–1973), martial arts expert

In 1609, a group of more than 100 Pilgrims boarded a wooden ship in England. They were looking for religious freedom. It took more than three months for the ship to arrive in America. Along the way, many people became ill, and one person died. Their first winter in America was also difficult. By the spring, less than 50 of the 100 people remained. These Pilgrims then met Native Americans. They wore little clothing, and what they wore was made from the hides of animals. They were dark-skinned, wore face paint, spoke different languages, and had a different culture. The Pilgrims from Europe were afraid of their differences with the Native Americans. Their fear was unnecessary. The Native Americans they met were peaceful. They helped the Europeans and taught them about the local plants and animals.

By 1621, at the first official Thanksgiving, the Pilgrims were getting used to their new home. They were living well. More Europeans arrived. Soon there were more whites than native peoples. More people meant that they needed more resources and more land. The Native Americans had the land and the resources. The two groups now found themselves fighting for land. The friendship between Native Americans and Europeans began to turn sour.

RED JACKET

When American colonists began to fight for their independence from the British Empire in 1775, the Iroquois people sided with the British. Many Americans wanted land owned by these Native Americans. The Native Americans hoped that the British would help them in land disputes with their white neighbors. However, when the American Revolutionary War was over in 1783, the Americans won, and the Native Americans and their white neighbors were no longer friends. Fights over resources and land in America continued.

In addition to fights over land to build homes, hunting grounds, and natural resources, the whites began to try to convert the Native Americans to the Christian religion. A popular Native American Seneca leader by the name of Red Jacket, or Sagoyewatha (Shay-go-ye-watha), tried to preserve his people's culture, religion, and land. He was a great speaker who used his words to help his people. In 1792, he met with George Washington and was given a peace medal for his work as a negotiator between the two groups. Still, the fighting continued, and in 1805, a Boston missionary society asked Red Jacket's permission to teach Christianity to the Iroquois people in New York State. Red Jacket politely refused.

In a famous speech, Red Jacket reminded the missionary society that when the Pilgrims came to America, "they found friends, and not enemies." His forefathers had told him that the Europeans had "come here to enjoy their religion." Red Jacket felt that the Native Americans' Great Spirit was the same as the Europeans' God. He wondered why all the whites did not agree on the same religion and rules because they all had access to the same Bible. In the end, he asked the missionary society to leave the Native Americans to their own culture. "Brother," he said, "we do not wish to destroy your religion, or take it from you; we only want to enjoy our

Red Jacket used his great oratory skills to help his fellow Native Americans preserve their land, religion, and culture. Although his original Native American name was Otetiani, he changed it to Sagoyewatha when he became a chief. That name roughly translates to "one who wakes them up."

own." Red Jacket wanted to have the same religious rights for his own people that the Pilgrims had come to America to preserve for themselves. A representative for the missionary society was furious and refused to shake Red Jacket's hand as he left. The push to convert Native Americans continued.

PRESERVING CULTURE

During the War of 1812 between America and England, the Native Americans chose the American side, but it was not the end of problems between the two groups. Fighting about land and culture continued. In 1819, President James Monroe sent a delegation called the Ogden Council to try to buy land from the Native Americans. The president wanted the Native Americans to sell their lands and move to a reservation.

General James Miller spoke for the Ogden Land Company and President Monroe. First he tried to stir the Native Americans' sense of culture. He said that their way of life was getting weaker. He tried to convince them that if they all moved closer together on a reservation, it would help them to keep their culture alive.

Midway through his speech, Miller began to threaten the Native Americans. He told them that the government would stop sending funds to support them. He said that white people would not sell them the supplies they needed to work their land. Miller compared the Native Americans to a great tree that had its roots deep in the earth and its branches reaching toward the clouds. Six Native American groups had as their symbol a white pine tree. Its roots spread in every direction, and it was a symbol of peace. Miller described the tree as losing its branches and rotting away. This wording was meant to express that President Monroe now saw the Native Americans as a dying people. He believed they were better off selling their lands and moving to a reservation.

Red Jacket replied that "the president must have been disordered in his mind" to ask them to leave. He wondered why, after the government and Native Americans had agreed to be friends, the tribes were now negotiating with land companies and hearing threats of a move to a reservation. Red Jacket looked around at the crowd of wealthy landowners at the meeting. He pointed to one man in particular who owned a lot of land. He said they should ask that man for some land because he had plenty. When the crowd laughed, Red Jacket continued: "Some here laugh. But do not think I trifle: I am sincere. Do not think we are hasty in making up our minds. We have had many councils, and thought for a long time upon this subject, and we will not part with any, not one of our reservations."

For about 40 years, Red Jacket gave speeches that helped his people. No other American figure had an influence on politics for that length of time. While his influence and leadership kept his culture and lands safe for a while, things were changing. Native Americans were eventually moved to reservations set up by the white government, but their culture and beliefs stayed intact.

NAVAJO CODE TALKERS

By 1860, white settlers had crossed the American plains, and they continued to push west. They met new groups of Native Americans, including the Navajo. The newcomers wanted the Native Americans off "their" land, and fighting broke out everywhere. During the Navajo War in 1860, the Native Americans fought for their lands and their way of life, but in 1864, they were finally defeated by U.S. Cavalry. The Navajo were exiled for four years to a reservation in New Mexico called Basque Redondo. Approximately 8,500 Navajo made the long walk to their new home. Then a treaty was signed, and a reservation was built on Navajo land, but only 6,000 Navajo people were alive to return.

The Navajo now had less land. They were forced to live closer together, and their herds of sheep and goats were smaller. Some of their children were forced to go to boarding schools run by English-speaking missionaries. If they spoke Navajo, their mouths were washed out with soap. Their land had been taken away. Now Navajo culture was being removed from their children's memories. However, the Navajo would later help the U.S. military and become heroes for speaking the very language the missionaries had once tried to take away.

In 1941, the Japanese attacked Pearl Harbor. The military base there was severely crippled. Many people lost their lives. Many ships, boats, and aircraft were destroyed. It was a surprise attack, and a great victory for the Japanese. Young men all over the United States rushed to enlist for war. Some of them were Navajo.

Despite being made into a minority in their own country and being looked down upon, the Navajo believed that America was their country. They believed that its government was their government. On June 3, 1940, the Navajo Tribal Council at Window Rock passed a resolution. It stated that the Navajo would be ready to defend the U.S. government against enemy forces. With the bombing at Pearl Harbor, the United States was pushed into World War II and the Navajo would get their chance to help.

Phillip Johnston had grown up among the Navajo as the son of a missionary. He had learned enough Navajo to be able to talk with them regularly. He knew that Comanche, another Native American language, had been used to transmit some codes during World War I. Since then, spies had been sent to the United States to learn every American language. Navajo was not one of them. It was too difficult to learn for someone who was not born into it. Johnston's idea was to create a code using Navajo words, but not the Navajo language. The words all together would not make any sense even to a native speaker.

Johnston was given the job of recruiting Navajo people. It was difficult because he needed people who spoke Navajo and English. Plus, many of the Navajo who wanted to join the fight had already enlisted right after Pearl Harbor was

Navajo code talkers played a major role in defending the United States in World War II despite facing oppression and prejudice at home. Above, Corporal Henry Bahe Jr. and Private First Class George H. Kirk, two code talkers serving with a Marine Signal Unit, operate a portable radio on the island of Bougainville in New Guinea (present-day Papua New Guinea) in 1943.

bombed. Finally, the military was able to recruit 29 Navajo men who then went through basic training. Because they had a special mission, they all were put together. These 29 men became the first all-Navajo platoon.

During basic training, they needed to adjust to some cultural differences. Navajo do not look people directly in the eye. They do not raise their voices to show authority. On the other hand, military drill sergeants often stare directly into recruits' eyes, and expect them to do the same. They also often shout at recruits. By the end of training, however, all 29 Navajo men were still there. Their commitment was unusual. Most military training platoons lose a few people during basic training.

The 29 new soldiers were asked to create a code based on an English word for each letter of the English language. For example, in the first code, *A* was *ant,* which was *wol-la-chee* in Navajo. The 29 soldiers then came up with alternate words

HONORING THE CODE TALKERS

On July 26, 2001, four of the original code talkers, and the son of one of them, stood in the Rotunda at the U.S. Capitol building. Around them were paintings of key moments in American history. One depicted the first Europeans to arrive in America; Native Americans were painted as part of the background. As in the paintings, these men had remained in the background for many years after World War II. Very few people knew about their contribution because the military kept it a secret. They were instructed never to talk about what they did because the code might be needed again. Sixty years later, the spotlight was finally focused on their heroism. The men were there to be presented with Congressional Medals of Honor by President George W. Bush.

In his speech, President Bush thanked the men. He described their service as "bravely offered and flawlessly performed." He noted that

that could be substituted for each letter and the Navajo words for those. They then used Navajo words to describe military things for which they would not have had words. In their code, bombs were given the Navajo word for "eggs," while grenades translated to the Navajo word for "potatoes." Even words for months were translated. April was called "small plant." Improvements to the code and additional words were added throughout the war.

The easiest part of the code was memorizing it. The Navajo language was spoken and had never been written down. Young Navajo children were used to memorizing everything they heard. The recruits had no trouble with this part.

The Navajo language that many had tried to erase ended up saving many lives during World War II. Furthermore, a group of people who had once been treated as enemies were able to forget the prejudice they endured to prove friendship.

400 Navajo had served as code talkers during the war and that 13 of them had lost their lives. He also reminded everyone that, besides these men, 44,000 other Native Americans fought as soldiers then, and many others continue to do so to this day.

President Bush credited Native American tradition for inspiring the men with "modesty and strength and quiet valor." He expressed gratefulness to them for coming forward to serve America despite the history of difficult conflicts between Native Americans and white Americans. Many people wonder why they would come forward to defend a country that treated them so poorly. Late in his life, one of the original code talkers, Albert Smith, revealed that their reason was in the code itself. The code word for America was "Our Mother."

SPADY KOYAMA

Spady Koyama was born in 1918 to Japanese parents in the United States. His father worked on a section gang as a railroad builder. When his father died, Spady and his siblings were sent to live with various family members in Japan. He was five years old. He lived with an aunt there until age 11. When he returned to the United States, he had to relearn English. He went to middle and high school in Spokane, Washington, where he considered himself American, not Japanese. "I sang just as loudly as any other kids, whenever we sang 'God Bless America,' or 'My Country 'Tis of Thee,' and I never thought of myself as anything but American," he said in 2005 in interviews for the Web site World War II His-

A young Spady Koyama poses with his family in this image taken circa 1940. Top row: brother Emo, brother Jack, Spady, and Spady's stepfather; Seated: stepsister Hannah, Spady's mother, and stepbrother Frank.

tory Class (www.wwiihistoryclass.com) and the magazine *Spokesman Review*.

Thus, when Pearl Harbor was bombed, Koyama felt like many young American men. He wanted to fight for his country. Koyama's Japanese-born mother came to his room right after the bombing and reminded him that the United States was his country, no matter what. Then she told him, half in English and half in Japanese, that he should join the army now that the United States was at war. However, she wanted him home for *kurisumasu* and *shougatsu*, which are the equivalents of "Christmas" and "New Year's." Koyama waited until January 5, 1942, to head to Spokane to enlist in the army.

When he arrived at the enlistment office, someone sitting at a desk pushed a piece of paper in front of him and asked him to sign it. When he did, the man looked at his name, and then looked up at him. He told Koyama that he had better go home. In his interview, Koyama recalled that the man said, "You know we're at war." Koyama responded that he knew that we were at war and that was why he had come to enlist for the army. The man would not process his paperwork. Koyama refused to leave. Finally, he pushed a piece of paper at the man and asked for his name and the names of every person in the office that day. He threatened to go to the newspaper with his story about not being allowed to join the army. The man buckled under the threat. Koyama raised his right hand and was sworn in to earn $21 a month as a private with the U.S. Army.

A little more than a month later, on February 19, 1942, President Franklin D. Roosevelt issued Executive Order 9066. It allowed the military to place Japanese Americans in internment camps. More than 110,000 men, women, and children were eventually removed from their homes and placed into camps. Some were citizens. Others were Japanese immigrants who were unable to become citizens due to the 1922 ruling in *Takao Ozawa v. U.S.* The law specifically denied anyone who was neither white nor black the right to become citizens. It targeted people of Asian descent. The law remained in place until 1952.

The Japanese Americans were taken to camps in Arkansas, Arizona, California, Idaho, Utah, and Oregon. The president and the military were concerned that any of these people could undermine their efforts in the war. They were also concerned that they may not have wanted to fight against people of their own culture. Koyama's mother packed a suitcase and waited for her evacuation order to arrive, but it never did.

Once he was in the army, Koyama interviewed for the Military Intelligence Service Language School. He graduated in June 1943 and was shipped out to Brisbane, Australia, to join the Allied Translator and Interpreter Section. Koyama says the graduates were separated into two groups. The ones who would not let someone take over a conversation were trained to be interrogators. They would question the enemy prisoners. The more quiet graduates were trained to be interpreters, or translators to try to break the enemy's code.

There were few Japanese Americans in the U.S. army, and their presence was kept quiet. They were supposed to be a surprise weapon against the Japanese, and yet many American soldiers did not realize that some of their allies looked like the enemy.

The Yankee Samurai

About a year after Executive Order 9066, Roosevelt realized that Japanese Americans like Koyama could be a great asset to the U.S. effort. The military attempted to recruit soldiers from the internment camps. Officials expected many men to sign up, but only 1,200 did. Most of these Japanese American soldiers served in Europe as part of the 442nd Regiment. A smaller number of soldiers, like Koyama, were selected to serve in the Pacific and became known as Yankee Samurai.

Koyama not only faced prejudicial treatment from fellow soldiers but also received it from the enemy. They did not seem to understand how a Japanese man could be part of

A SENATOR REMINDS U.S. OF DISCRIMINATION

On September 11, 2001, three groups of men of Arabic descent flew passenger airplanes into the Twin Towers in New York City and the Pentagon building in Washington, D.C. A fourth plane crashed outside of Pennsylvania and never reached its target. Shortly afterward, a wave of anti-Arab discrimination passed over the United States. Two weeks after the attack, a pollster conducted a survey and found that nearly a third of the people polled would have allowed Arab-American citizens to be held for questioning. Muslim leaders across the country were very concerned.

Senator Daniel K. Inouye knew all about this kind of discrimination. He was alive when the Japanese attacked Pearl Harbor. In fact, he became a member of the famous 442nd Regimental Combat Team that fought during World War II as the Yankee Samurai, and later lost his right arm due to a grenade explosion.

The National Japanese American Memorial was opened in Washington, D.C., in 2001 to honor Japanese Americans who fought in World War II. Representative Robert Matsui of California, Secretary of Transportation Norman Mineta, and Senator Daniel Inouye of Hawaii cut the ribbon to open the memorial.

(continues)

(continued)

In 1962, he became a senator of Hawaii, his home state. In a 2001 *New York Times Magazine* interview, the senator said that the results of the survey reminded him of the days just after Pearl Harbor. President Franklin D. Roosevelt's executive order considered all Japanese to be "enemy aliens." About 120,000 Japanese Americans were evacuated. Inouye had learned from a national security expert that about 600 Muslims had been held right after the September 11 attacks. No charges were brought against them. It was much less than the 120,000 Japanese Americans held in 1941, but to Inouye, it was still unacceptable. However, he was happy to see that President George W. Bush stood up for Muslims and for tolerance.

In Washington, D.C., a memorial to the Japanese Americans who fought in World War II was built. On the opening panel, there is a warning: "The lessons learned must remain as a grave reminder of what we must not allow to happen again to any group." Those words were Daniel Inouye's. After September 11, 2001, it seemed that some people still had that lesson to learn.

the U.S. Army. One day, Koyama was assigned to interrogate a Japanese officer. He went into the room with the man and explained in Japanese what they were going to talk about. He noticed that the Japanese officer looked more and more angry the longer Koyama spoke. When he was finished, the Japanese officer leaned forward and spat in Koyama's face. Koyama yelled at him in Japanese and spat back. The Japanese officer got scared. A Japanese officer would never have spoken to him or acted toward him that way. The prisoner knew right then that he was dealing with an American.

Shortly after Koyama had proven himself with this interview, he was stationed in New Guinea for a few months, where he interrogated prisoners. Then Koyama was shipped off to the Philippines. On the way there, on October 25, 1944,

Veteran Army Colonel Spady Koyama poses proudly in uniform. His medals represent service through three wars: World War II, the Korean Conflict, and the Vietnam War. He was also given a Purple Heart for wounds sustained during World War II.

Fifty-five years after the end of World War II, the nation's top honor for bravery on the battlefield was awarded to 22 Asian-American veterans. Above, President Bill Clinton presents the Congressional Medal of Honor to Private George T. Sakato of the 442nd Regimental Combat Team in 2000.

enemy dive-bombers attacked the ship he was on. Koyama was hit with ricocheted pieces of shrapnel. When he woke up, he was lying on a beach with nearly 30 other men. He worried about being out in the open, where anyone could see them. Plus, he could not tell what his injuries were. There was blood in his right eye, so he could not see out of it. He thought that he might have lost that eye. He reached up to feel his left ear and was happy to find it still in place. Instead of putting his hand back to his side, he laid it across his chest. This small action may have saved him. Some soldiers nearby noticed that he was the only one with his hand across his chest. They went over to him and realized that he was alive. Koyama thought he was in a group of wounded soldiers waiting to be examined by doctors. In fact, he was in a group waiting to be buried. Koyama was placed on a stretcher and taken to a hospital.

There, he was given a Purple Heart medal. These are awarded to people who have been wounded in the line of duty. Koyama tried to look as well as he could as he waited for the general to pin his medal on his uniform. Yet, when Koyama's name was called, the general stopped abruptly. He seemed confused. The person reading out the names assured the general that Koyama was an American, "one of us." Once again, Koyama felt he was being judged only by the way he looked. He was angered by the general's reaction and waited to see what would happen, but the general simply pinned on the medal and moved to the next person on the list.

When Koyama was finally released from the hospital a year later, he returned home to Spokane. There, he read a newspaper report that said the Spokane chapter of the Veterans of Foreign Wars (VFW) would not allow a Japanese-American, one of the 442nd unit, to become a member. The VFW chapter felt that other veterans who fought in World War II against the Japanese would be upset by a Japanese-American member. Koyama wanted to expose their injustice. He applied to be a member. He invited the press as well. His actions embarrassed the VFW in front of the entire United States. He went on to give speeches around the Spokane area about his experience in the Pacific War and what happened with the VFW. Later, the VFW asked him to become a member. He turned them down.

Koyama returned to services in 1949 and was an officer in the Korean Conflict and Vietnam War. After he retired from the army, he helped start a retired officers' association. Koyama's unit, the 442nd Regimental Combat Team, which was composed entirely of Japanese Americans, came to be known as the most decorated in the history of the U.S. Army.

In 2000, there was some question as to why so many decorated officers were in Spady's unit, but only one Congressional Medal of Honor had been awarded. The investigation found that many men had qualified for the honor but were never awarded it. In June of 2000, President Bill Clinton awarded 22 veterans the Congressional Medal of Honor. Some were awarded to men who had already died, either in the line of duty or afterward, since it had been many years since they had fought. Once again, the wrongs of prejudice were made right.

PLAYING TO WIN

3

> "If we cannot come together as a human
> race, forget about the team."
>
> —Herman Boone (1935–),
> coach of the 1971 Titans football team

Just as Native Americans and Japanese Americans struggled to find equality in America, African Americans have also dealt with prejudice. In the mid-1800s to until about the late 1960s, they faced the practice of segregation, or separation, particularly in the southern states where slavery was once part of the economy. In this case, racial prejudice was used to separate people by skin color. In the nineteenth century, a popular but stereotypical song-and-dance act featured an African-American character called Jim Crow. Jim Crow was actually a white man in blackface makeup whose character belittled African Americans. Laws in the South that legally kept the races apart soon came to be known as Jim Crow laws. This form of segregation continued through all areas of life, even sports.

PLAYING AT HOME

In the early 1800s, an English bat-and-ball game called "rounders" made its way to the United States. New York City firefighter Alexander Joy Cartwright played a version of it called "town ball" in a vacant lot. When the lot became unavailable, he and some other players moved to Elysian Fields in Hoboken, New Jersey. In order to pay the rental fees for the park, Cartwright formed a team. He named it after his firehouse. This is how the baseball team the New York Knickerbockers got its name. The foremost rule was that every player "should have the reputation of a gentleman."

This gentleman's game became "America's pastime" by the late 1800s. The minor-league Toledo Blue Stockings signed Moses Fleetwood "Fleet" Walker to play on its team. Walker was African American. In 1883, Walker was scheduled to play a game against future Hall-of-Famer Cap Anson. Anson said he would not play with Walker on the field because of Walker's race. The Blue Stockings' manager, Charlie Morton, put Walker in the game anyway. He told Anson's team, the Chicago White Stockings, that they would not get their share of the gate money if they did not play the game. Anson decided to play.

The following year, in 1884, Toledo became a major-league team. Walker became the first African-American major-league player. Yet, racism still plagued him, even from his own teammates. Blue Stockings pitcher Tony Mullane said Walker "was the best catcher I ever worked with, but I disliked a Negro and whenever I had to pitch to him I used to pitch anything I wanted without looking at his signals."

After an injury, Walker left the Blue Stockings. In 1887, he began to play for a minor league team, the Little Giants, in the International League. On July 14 of that year, the International League owners voted to ban African-American players from the game. Walker was too good to ignore, so an exception was made for him, and he was moved to a team in Syracuse, New York.

He then faced Anson and the Chicago White Stockings for a second time. This time Walker's new team did not back him up. Syracuse replaced Walker as pitcher and the game continued. A couple of years later, both leagues, the Ameri-

Moses Fleetwood Walker *(no. 6, middle row, left)* and his brother Weldy *(no. 10, top row, second from right)* became the first and second African Americans to play professional baseball when they played for Toledo, which was a major-league team in 1884. Above, the men pose in 1881 as part of the first varsity baseball team of Oberlin College in Ohio.

can Association and the National League, unofficially banned African-American players. The ban stayed in place for 57 years.

With the ban in place, there was nowhere for talented African-American players to go. They formed a league of their own.

AWAY GAMES

Baseball teams made up of only African-American players began 20 years before the unwritten ban was established. In

1865, black baseball teams began to dominate the sport. At first, they even played all-white teams. In 1867, the promoter of an all-black team attempted to apply for membership in the National Association of Base Ball Players. The association decided to exclude "any club which may be composed of one of more colored players."

By the early 1900s, all-black teams had been formed all over the United States. Because there were not enough teams to play against, ball clubs had to travel to Mexico and Puerto Rico for games. African-American players did not make as much money as white players. Plus, when they traveled to the South, they were treated poorly because of Jim Crow laws. Despite the challenges, the players on these teams continued

Under the Jim Crow laws, African Americans could not drink from the same water fountain as white people. Above, a man drinks from a segregated water fountain in Oklahoma City, OK, in 1939.

to do well. Many of them were excellent players, and soon, owners of all-white teams started to notice.

PLAYING TOGETHER

In 1945, the Major League Committee on Baseball Integration was formed. One of its members, Larry MacPhail, was a critic of integration, or the mixing of races. He made sure that the committee never met. However, Branch Rickey, another member, was committed to integrating baseball. He knew that there were plenty of good athletes in the Negro Leagues. He did not see any reason why they should not be allowed to play in the majors. Yet, he knew that other people would not see it the same way, so he pretended that he wanted to start a new Negro League team. He sent scouts all over the United States, Mexico, and Puerto Rico to find the best ballplayers in the Negro League. By August of that year, his scouts had identified three people: Roy Campanella, Don Newcombe, and Jackie Robinson.

On August 28, 1945, Robinson and Rickey met in Rickey's Brooklyn office. Robinson was expecting to be asked to join a new team called the Brooklyn Brown Dodgers. He was surprised when Rickey told him that he wanted him to play in the major leagues. Their meeting lasted three hours. During the meeting, Rickey gave Robinson a test. He wanted to make sure that Robinson would be able to stand up to the kind of negative treatment he would get as the only black player on a white team. He shouted at Robinson and called him names. Robinson was confused. "Mr. Rickey," he asked, "do you want a ballplayer who's afraid to fight back?" Rickey responded, "I want a player with guts enough not to fight back." He explained that he wanted Robinson "to do this job with base hits and stolen bases and by fielding the ground balls. Nothing else."

For years, bigoted sportswriters had said that African Americans did not have enough talent and could not play as well as white players. However, Rickey had seen the talent for himself, and he wanted to build a winning team. He

Jackie Robison signs a contract in 1945 with Dodgers owner Branch Rickey, becoming the first African-American player in the modern era of Major League Baseball.

knew that he had to get the best African-American players, but there was a lot at stake. People who were against integration would be waiting for failure. If Robinson got angry, or lashed out, Rickey knew that people would look at it as a failure of integration. According to Ken Rappoport's book *Profiles in Sports Courage*, Rickey said, "One incident, just one incident, can set it back 20 years." Robinson wondered if people would think he was weak and if he could really let his performance on the field speak for itself. Finally, he said, "Mr. Rickey, I think I can play ball in Brooklyn. If you want to take this gamble, I promise you there will be no incident."

Robinson was signed to play with the Montreal Royals. They were a farm team for the Brooklyn Dodgers. Farm teams were the minor leagues. If players did well there, they would be moved to the majors. From the Royals, Robinson would move to the major-league Dodgers.

THE LIFE OF JACKIE ROBINSON

Jackie Robinson was born in Cairo, Georgia, in 1919 to Jerry and Mallie Robinson. He was the grandson of slaves. Although slavery had been abolished, conditions for African Americans in the South were still very hard. Robinson's parents were sharecroppers. Sharecroppers worked a section of farm that belonged to a white landowner. They bought their supplies on credit. At the end of the year, when the crop was sold, the landowner took a percentage of the profits. Then he took out what the sharecroppers owed on credit. Most sharecroppers ended the year still owing money. Sharecropping was a hard life. Jerry Robinson was frustrated with his life and left Mallie and their five children. Mallie packed up the children and left for Pasadena, California. She lived with a brother until she could find work and a home of her own.

Pasadena was divided by race. White families and black families lived in separate parts of town. When Robinson was only three years old, his mother, her sister, and her brother-in-law managed to save up enough money to buy a house. They bought it in a white neighborhood.

The neighbors were not welcoming. They tried many times to get the family to move. A cross was burned on their front lawn. The police were called because one neighbor was afraid. Rocks were thrown. Still, Mallie Robinson refused to leave Pepper Street. In time, the neighbors changed. Other black, Hispanic, and Asian families moved in. The Robinsons were not alone any more.

Jackie Robinson was an average student but an outstanding athlete. He played baseball, basketball, and tennis and ran track. His older brother, Mack, was a track star who went to the 1936 Olympics and returned home with a gold and a silver medal. These Olympic games were a victory, not just over the other athletes, but also over Nazi Germany. Germany

ASHE AGAINST APARTHEID

Arthur Ashe grew up in Richmond, Virginia, in the 1960s. Richmond was segregated. Ashe could not play tennis on courts with white players. He had to travel miles away to practice. Ashe's father was a local police officer who taught his children never to make enemies and that people gain by helping others. His father's lessons taught him to always stand up for others.

Ashe was invited to attend Sumner High School in Missouri where he did not have to travel far to play. At Sumner, he won the National Junior Indoor Tennis Championship and was an honor student. Then the University of California at Los Angeles gave him a grant to play tennis for them. Later that year, he also became the first African-American member of the United States Davis Cup team.

In 1968, at the first U.S. Open, Ashe won the men's title. He wanted to go along with the Davis Cup team to play in the South African Open. The government of South Africa denied him a visa to enter their country. South Africa had apartheid laws. *Apartheid* is a word from the Afrikaans language. It means "apartness." Apartheid was legal racism. Laws were set up that favored whites in the country and disfavored blacks. Ashe went to the media and demanded that South Africa be expelled from the International Lawn Tennis Federation. That never happened, but three years later, Ashe was granted a visa and allowed to play. He believed that he could help break down the barriers of apartheid by proving that a black person could play well.

In 1977, 50 American groups came together to protest apartheid and boycott South African sports. Ashe opposed their ban. He felt that the way to show that integration could work was to go there and play. After returning from South Africa, Ashe decided to speak to the protesters. Richard Lapchick, who was also a tennis player, was leading the group. He was afraid that Ashe would convince the protesters to leave.

was the host country. Its leader, Adolf Hitler, believed that certain kinds of white people were superior to everyone else. These people were called Aryans. Mack Robinson's and other

Arthur Ashe is the first African American ever to win the men's singles titles at Wimbledon, the U.S. Open, and the Australian Open. Above, Ashe waves to fans after winning the men's title in 1975 at Wimbledon, while the Duke of Kent applauds in front of him.

When Ashe came out, however, he told the assembled group that he had been wrong.

Ashe told them that he tried to buy tickets to a match for some kids in South Africa. They were sent to an "Africans-only" counter. He realized then that the boycott was the only way to stop apartheid. He joined the group right then and there. Ashe convinced other tennis players, such as John McEnroe, to join the boycott. Apartheid officially ended 15 years later, in 1991.

African-Americans' victories over German and other white athletes were also victories over racism.

Back at home, Robinson went to UCLA and lettered in four sports. He also met his future wife, Rachel Isum. After graduation, Robinson served in the armed forces from 1942 to 1944. Serving as an officer in the Deep South was difficult. Toward the end of his time there, he rode a bus from the army base into town. The bus driver told Robinson to sit at the back of the bus. That was where African Americans were supposed to sit. Robinson refused. As a soldier, he could sit anywhere he liked. Robinson argued with another officer outside of the bus and was arrested. He was sent to military court, but the charges were dismissed. Not long after, Robinson decided to leave the army.

He returned to the Negro Leagues, where the salaries were lower than the major leagues and the schedules were not structured. When the teams traveled to the South, they had to follow Jim Crow laws. The Negro Leagues had showcased great players such as Satchel Paige, Josh Gibson, Willie Mays, Hank Aaron, and Robinson. Yet, these players had little hope that they would ever be able to play in the majors. Then along came Branch Rickey and his idea to integrate baseball.

The Majors

Once Robinson was signed to play with the Montreal Royals, he and his wife went to the Royals' training camp in Florida. Normally, Rickey did not invite players' wives, but he made an exception for Robinson. The Robinsons' experience began badly. First they had to give up their seats on the plane. Then they had to wait 12 hours for another flight. Because they were in the South, they were not allowed to eat in the coffee shop. Fortunately, Robinson's mother, who was from the South, had anticipated problems. She packed the couple some food that got them through the day. They finally arrived at spring training, and there were reporters from all over the

United States waiting with questions. They wanted to know what Robinson would do if pitchers threw at his head. "Duck," he replied. After practice, the white players went to a nearby hotel. Robinson, his wife, and other black sportswriters had to go to a black community and stay in a motel or in someone's home. They even had to eat their meals apart from the rest of the team. Robinson's wife never left his side. Still, by the end of that year, Robinson was Brooklyn-bound.

Robinson was already 28 years old. He was hardly a newcomer, but he was a major-league rookie. The door was now open for more African-American players to join the majors. Many people were happy. Many others were upset. In the Dodger locker room, some players made a petition against him. It stated that if Robinson came to the team, they would request to be traded. Robinson was to play shortstop, and the other players approached the current shortstop to sign as well. It was Pee Wee Reese. Reese was from the South. He was from a family that believed in segregation, but he did not sign the petition. "If he can take my job," he said, "he's entitled to it." Soon, the Dodgers manager heard about the players' petition. He told them that he did not care what color Robinson was, or even if he had stripes like a zebra. "I'm the manager of this team," Rickey said, "and I say he plays." It was the end of the petition.

After a few games, Robinson won over his teammates. By the time they went to Philadelphia to play the Phillies, they were happy that he was part of the team. Their belief in him was about to be put to the test. Phillies manager Ben Chapman yelled insults at Robinson throughout the game. He told Robinson to go back to the South. He said he was only good for picking cotton and cleaning out toilets. The Phillies players followed their manager's lead and yelled insults, too. The insults were so loud and terrible and persistent that the Dodgers teammates were outraged. Even those who had signed the petition against Robinson were now backing him up. Even Phillies fans who were sitting close to the dugout wrote complaint letters about Chapman's behavior to the commissioner of baseball.

The Dodgers manager played Robinson in the first-base position. He was not used to the position, but he did not

COACHING IN BLACK AND WHITE

In 1971, schools were beginning to integrate. That meant that schools were now accepting students from every race. In Alexandria, Virginia, three schools were coming together. Not only were they segregated, but they were also football rivals.

Bill Yoast, the head coach of one of the three schools, was favored to coach the new team at T.C. Williams High School. Instead of Yoast, Herman Boone, an African American, was chosen. Yoast became the assistant coach. Together, Boone and Yoast worked to make the team push past their racial differences and their old school rivalries. In a 2007 interview, Boone said, "I knew the entire city was watching me like a lion in the bush watching a gazelle." They were waiting for him to make a mistake so that they could pounce. At the team's first practice, he made the players all shake hands. And when the team left for a two-week football camp, all the white players went on one bus, and all the black players went on another one. Boone made them all travel together. The players did not speak to each other on the ride, but they said that it was "stressful."

Things were stressful for Boone as well. One night someone threw a toilet through the window of his house. He said that the incident motivated him.

He felt that communication was the key to bring the team together. So he encouraged them to talk. Then Boone took the players to the Soldiers National Cemetery at Gettysburg, Pennsylvania. He wanted to show how two sides of an issue could destroy people. By the end of the two weeks, the players felt comfortable with each other. They ate together and joked with each other. Then they went on to have an undefeated season and win the 1971 state football championship.

In 2000, actor Denzel Washington starred in a movie based on Boone's experiences. It is called *Remember the Titans*.

complain. As players rounded first base, they used the spikes under their shoes to stamp at Robinson's foot. Some spat on him. They yelled insults. Still, Robinson did not fight back. His playing got better and better, and the Dodgers were heading toward winning the National League pennant. Yet, at a game in Cincinnati, the actions of the fans became intolerable. They booed and cursed at him. Finally, Pee Wee Reese, the short-stop who had refused to sign the petition, called a time-out. He walked over to Robinson and put his hand on Robinson's shoulder. He stood like that for a few moments just talking to him. His actions calmed Robinson down. More importantly, it showed the fans that Robinson was an accepted member of the Dodgers. The taunts stopped.

After the Dodgers won the pennant, Robinson was named Rookie of the Year by *Sporting News*. That same newspaper had once opposed integration and claimed, "There is not a single Negro player with major-league possibilities."

With Robinson proving himself as a major-league player, other African-American ballplayers were signed to the Dodgers, and many other ball clubs decided to integrate. His success inspired integration in other sports. The National Basketball Association and the National Football League began to sign African-American players as well. Robinson became a hero to many African Americans. His willingness to be nonviolent, to suffer quietly, and to stand up for what he knew was right helped bring an end to years of established prejudice in sports. Seven years after he helped to integrate sports, the Supreme Court decided to integrate U.S. schools.

SEPARATE EDUCATION

"The highest result of education is tolerance."

—Helen Keller (1880–1968),
first deaf and blind person to graduate from college

Integrating schools proved to be even more difficult than integrating sports. A legal precedent from 1896 supported educational racism. In 1896, the *Plessy v. Ferguson* Supreme Court case stated that black and white students should attend separate schools. However, the schools had to be equal: Equal in the type of education they provided, equal in their facilities, and equal in the materials provided to the students. After separate schools were built, it became clear that nothing about them was equal. White students had better facilities and materials, which translated into a better education and the ability to get into good colleges. Black students often had little or no supplies, faced poor conditions in their schools, and ultimately lacked the level of education necessary to get into a good college. The system was set up to continue racial prejudice against some students and deny them the right to a good education. The system needed to be changed.

BROWN V. BOARD OF EDUCATION

Several parents in Topeka, Kansas, sued the Board of Education there to change the "separate-but-equal" ruling. Their case was named *Brown v. Board of Education* for one of the fathers in the group and an assistant pastor, Oliver L. Brown. The parents ultimately lost. Thurgood Marshall, the parents' attorney who later became a Supreme Court judge, then combined the *Brown* lawsuit with several other lawsuits from around the country into a civil suit. The case was scheduled to go before the Supreme Court, with Fred M. Vinson as chief justice.

Vinson believed in the separate-but-equal law. Marshall and the parents behind the suit had little hope that they would win. Events turned when Vinson died and President Dwight D. Eisenhower chose the governor of California, Earl Warren, as the new chief justice. Warren was well liked and considered a conservative. Still, Chief Justice Warren ruled that separate was *not* in fact equal. Schools were to be desegregated immediately. While the black community cheered, Eisenhower said he regretted giving Warren the job.

FAUBUS VS. EISENHOWER

Many southern states began immediate desegregation plans. They believed that the decision of the highest court must be followed. Others did it based solely on economics. It cost a lot of money to run separate schools, especially in northern states where there were fewer black students. In Arkansas, desegregation plans began immediately but then stalled. Governor Orval Faubus did not take a stand on desegregation in the beginning. When he was running for reelection, he realized that the people of Arkansas mostly favored segregation. He then did everything in his power to stop schools from desegregating.

The NAACP (National Association for the Advancement of Colored People) asked the school board in Arkansas to allow

Conservative Chief Justice of the United States Supreme Court Earl Warren, seen here in the 1960s, called for the desegregation of schools.

black students to attend the mostly white high schools. The NAACP even helped black students to write applications to these schools, but the students were always turned down. In March 1957, the head of the school board picked 17 students to integrate. He felt that they were the least likely to cause any trouble. Over the course of the summer, eight of the volunteers decided not to go. Nine were left.

The day before the nine were to start school at Little Rock Central High School, Governor Faubus called in the National Guard to prevent the students from entering their new school. Daisy Bates, the head of the local NAACP, called eight of the nine that night and set up a meeting place with them. She arranged for a black minister and a white minister to accompany them to school the next morning. One student did not have a phone and so did not get the message.

On the morning of September 24, 1957, 15-year-old Elizabeth Eckford dressed for school. In a starched white shirtdress and dark glasses, she headed off alone. "I did not expect any violence," she said in a 2007 interview on National Public Radio. When she got to Central High, the National Guard was there, as well as a mob of about 100 white people. Eckford strode on toward the school, but men with guns barred her path. They were allowing only white students to pass. "It wasn't until the National Guard directed me across the street to those angry people that I realized they were there solely to keep me from going to school."

National reporters from *Time* magazine were also blocked from approaching the scene and were later beaten and arrested. Only one reporter, Will Counts, made it close enough to see what was happening. Counts was a local man who had attended Central High. He worked for the *Arkansas Gazette*, and that morning he purposely dressed in a flannel shirt to better blend in with the crowd. He was present as Eckford was turned away from three entrances to the school. She looked into the crowd, searching for a familiar or friendly face. She thought at least an adult would help her, but the one woman she looked at spat on her. She began to walk away, and the mob followed. Counts snapped photos of the incident, capturing the contorted, angry face of Hazel Bryan Massery hurling insults at Eckford.

"I think we were saying, 'Go home,'" Massery said in a 1997 interview in the *Chicago Tribune*. Yet, her words were

Elizabeth Eckford, one of the nine African-American students who were integrated into Little Rock's Central High School in 1957, ignores the angry shouts and stares of fellow students, including Hazel Bryan Massery *(behind Eckford's left shoulder)*, on her first day of school.

apparently more malicious than she remembers. "I never repeat what she said," Eckford said in a 2000 *Chicago Tribune* interview. "It hurts me today."

Eckford made her way to a bus stop, where a white reporter from the *New York Times* encouraged her not to cry, and a white woman sat next to her and tried to console her. Eventually, one of the students and an adult helped Eckford onto a bus and to her safety. She rode to the School for the Blind, where her mother worked. When she got there, her mother was in the basement laundry room. She had heard false reports about her daughter being injured by a mob on the radio. She had her back to the door and did not see her daughter come in. She was praying.

It took three weeks of attempts before the nine students were finally allowed into the school for good. President Eisenhower exchanged a few tense telegrams with Governor Faubus. He tried to force Faubus to integrate. Faubus refused. The two eventually met face to face, but Faubus would not back down. Eisenhower did not intervene until Counts's pictures of Eckford appeared in newspapers around the world.

Eisenhower took over the National Guard and had local police escort the students into the school. By then, the mob outside the school had grown from about 100 on the first day to about 1,000. Daisy Bates from the NAACP sent some black reporters on ahead. The mob attacked them, thinking that they were the students, while the police escorted the actual students inside. The white students were surprised to see the Little Rock Nine inside the school building. Some of them were so afraid that they jumped out of second-floor windows.

Nine vs. 1,900

Ernest Green, the first of the nine to graduate, believed things would get better. He was mistaken. He later said that a small number of students had conducted a "reign of terror" on the nine black students. In addition to enduring daily harassment, there were several exceptional incidents: Melba Pattillo Beals had acid thrown in her eyes and was pelted with raw eggs. Her New Year's resolution for 1958 was to do her best to stay alive until the last day of school. Eckford was pushed down a flight of stairs. Minnijean Brown Trickey had ink and soup spilled on her. Jefferson Thomas was pelted with a rock and knocked unconscious. Both Green and Terrence Roberts were kicked and punched. All were tripped, spat on, had books knocked out of their arms, and were called racial slurs. The only one who escaped most of the torment was Thelma Mothershed Wair. She had a bad heart, so everyone left her alone.

Each morning, Minnijean Brown Trickey chose her clothes carefully, wondering what kind of stain they would have by the end of the day. Eventually she got fed up. During one lunch period, she noticed some of the white girls smirking and whispering. She sensed something was about to happen. As she walked over to where the other black students were eating, there was kicking and shoving in front of her. It was the last straw. She dropped her chili on a white boy sitting nearby. In a 2007 interview for *USA Today*, she said that the act immediately ruined her life. She was suspended, and later on, after more run-ins with segregationists, she was expelled. Some students handed out cards that read, "ONE DOWN... EIGHT TO GO." None of the white students were ever punished.

White students also were affected by what was happening. Dent Gitchell was the boy on which Brown Trickey spilled her chili. He said that he had never had contact with her before and was confused by the actions around him. He was also on the softball field when Thomas was attacked with a rock during practice. The coach told the team that behavior like that was not to be tolerated, but his smirk sent a different message.

Josh McHughes was a star of Central's championship football team that year. He passed Eckford in the hallway every day and later said that she always looked terrified. He never said anything to her then, and 50 years later, even though they sometimes work in the same building, he says he still cannot think of what to say.

Ralph Brodie, who was student body president in 1957, is angered by the way the media depicted the white students of the school. "I'm sure they were bullied," he said of the nine black students in an interview for *USA Today* in 2007. "But that's history." He saw that whites that supported segregation were threatened. "When there are people you know who are having those problems," he said, "You got to mind your own business, and that's what most of us did."

The first black students integrated into the then all-white Little Rock Central High School in 1957 pose in front of the school forty years later. They are *(from left)*: Carlotta Walls LaNier, Melba Pattillo Beals, Terrence Roberts, Gloria Ray Karlmark, Thelma Mothershed Wair, Ernest Green, Elizabeth Eckford, Minnijean Brown Trickey, and Jefferson A. Thomas.

Eckford wholeheartedly disagrees. She thinks that the ones who minded their own business were part of the problem. "All of the students who said, that we see nowadays,

RETURN TO LITTLE ROCK

On the 40th anniversary of integration in Little Rock, Arkansas, Elizabeth Eckford and Hazel Bryan Massery met for the first time since they left school. In 1963, Massery had called Eckford to offer her apologies for insulting her in that famous photo, and Eckford graciously accepted. This time, it was Will Counts, the photographer who had taken the original picture of them in 1957, who got the two women together. He took their photo again and titled it "Reconciliation." Eckford and Massery went on to give speeches together, talking to schools about their experiences and appearing on talk shows for about four years. After that, Massery stopped talking to Eckford. Like many of the citizens of Little Rock, Massery did not see the benefit of continuing to relive the past. She has refused to give interviews since 2001. "In the end, there was no reconciliation," Eckford has said.

Yet, today in Central High, the results of the nine's efforts are clear. It is now a fully integrated school. The senior prom is fully integrated even as other southern high schools still struggle with the idea of an integrated dance. Hispanic and Asian students now make up the minority at Central High. In teacher Nancy Wilson's art class, the students interact freely, discussing and criticizing each other's work. But in the lunchroom, students still segregate themselves. They attribute this separation to the natural desire to be with others who share similar interests. In an article for *USA Today* titled "After 40 Years, a Return to Central High," African-American senior Angela Moore said, "People just naturally gravitate toward those whom they have more in common with." Crystal Brooks, a white junior, explains, "Just because two white friends choose to sit with one another doesn't mean they're being racist." The fact that friendships sometimes break down along color lines is neither a surprise nor a concern to Central High students today.

that say they went to school there? Say, 'Wasn't me, wasn't me. I wasn't one of those attacking you.'" She went on to say, "People around me that I saw didn't react to what they saw or what they had to have heard. They turned their backs," she said in a CNN interview in 2004. Today when Eckford gives speeches to students, she encourages them to stand up and do something. She tells them that they can be somebody's hope. She tells them that being a silent witness is like telling the harassers it is okay to do what they are doing.

Green and the other students were able to identify 55 students who tormented them out of the school's 1,900 students. Of the vast majority of other students, a few tried to befriend their black classmates, but they and their families were subject to social and economic pressure. Fortunately for Eckford, at least two students and their families did not succumb to the pressure. One of them was Ken Reinhardt. He talked to her all the time, even though he was beaten up often for doing so. He said that he knew it was the right thing to do. Another was Ann Williams. Her family had to have an armed guard at their house because she befriended Eckford. Williams's father was the head of the Little Rock Chamber of Commerce in 1958, and he supported integration openly. Many years later, at an event honoring Williams's father, Eckford stood up to tell him how his daughter had reached out to her. Everyone was startled at this show of emotion from Eckford, who was usually shy and reserved. Eckford did not even know the hardships that the family endured because of their support of integration at the time. Her friend never told her.

SEPARATION VS. INCLUSION

Integrating schools is not just a black and white issue. It is also about the abled and disabled. Up to the early 1970s, more than one million children in the United States had no access to public education. Another 3.5 million were placed in segregated facilities. These facilities provided little or no effective instruction. Students were segregated based on disabilities. Those who were blind, deaf, "emotionally disturbed," or "mentally retarded" had to attend separate schools.

All of this changed in 1974 when Congress passed the Education for All Handicapped Children Act (EHA), which later became the Individuals with Disabilities Education Act (IDEA). It made sure that children with disabilities could get a free public education. Anyone from birth to age 21 was eligible if they were considered disabled. Their education had to accomplish at least one of three goals: to get them ready for more education, to prepare them for a job, or to teach

A GOOD IDEA

About the same time that African-American students were fighting for their right to attend better schools, parents of children with disabilities were fighting to get their children a proper education. Many children with disabilities used to be put into institutions. There, they got the bare minimum in clothing, food, and shelter. No one tried to determine the extent of their abilities or disabilities. Little or nothing was taught. The Office of Special Education reported that there were some children who were worse off in the institutions than they would have been in their own homes. They told the story of one person who was brought to the institution as an infant. He was smart but emotionally disabled. Over many years, he copied the actions of other students and began to injure himself. This behavior caused him to go blind. By the time he was properly evaluated, he was over 35 years old.

Parents demanded that the government provide better services. A series of court cases followed. And finally, the federal government responded. In the 1950s and 1960s, legislation was passed that improved programs and services for students with disabilities. The legislation ensured that teachers would get proper training to educate students with special needs.

The institutions were expensive, so parents tried to get their children into regular public schools. In 1975, the Education for All Handicapped them life skills so that they could live on their own. By the mid-1980s, integrated programs for students with disabilities were having success around the country. Students were getting the education that they needed based on their individual needs. Students were no longer segregated based on ability. However, the debate seemed to rage on about the best way to educate students, and some families were caught up in the struggle.

In 1985, Lynn Robison and her parents were prepared for her to enter kindergarten. Lynn had been diagnosed with

Children Act (EHA) was passed. It meant that the more than one million children with disabilities in the United States who were not getting any education now had the right to a free public education.

In 1997, the act was renamed the Individuals with Disabilities Education Act (IDEA). In addition to a free education, IDEA ensures that students can attend a neighborhood school. This is called inclusion. Inclusion has been defined as rejecting segregation for any reason. The words of the judge in *Brown v. Board of Education* had helped to set the tone for IDEA. Parents prefer inclusion because it promotes acceptance. Inclusion helps students feel like part of their school community. This acceptance in turn helps them to be more social, and many parents report that their children are happier because of it. However, just as the Little Rock Nine were not welcomed into their school community, many students with disabilities and their families face the same kind of rejection. Some parents of general-education students resist the inclusion of students with disabilities in classes with their own children. Some districts try to pull students with disabilities out of general-education classes and put them into special programs. This form of prejudice, called "ableism," continues to hinder students and their families from being included, without question, in all classrooms across the United States.

cerebral palsy. Her speech was difficult to understand, and she did not have the same physical abilities as her other classmates. However, Lynn's parents wanted her to attend regular public school. Under IDEA, she was eligible to attend a regular neighborhood school. Lynn was not able to do everything her fellow students did, but the school helped her to adapt. Her classroom teacher worked well with her. In addition, a special teacher was assigned to her. That teacher helped Lynn and adapted her work. Lynn was able to take the same tests that her classmates did. Her parents said the most important outcome was for Lynn to make friends.

Lynn was a pioneer. With her success, other parents of special-needs students in the area found out about enrolling their children in regular public schools. Then, without warning, things changed. In the summer before Lynn began third grade, the school board designated one school for all students with severe disabilities. Lynn fell under that category. She was going to be moved out of her classroom and away from her friends. The new facility was about 10 miles away. Parents of these severely disabled students tried to understand the district's sudden change of heart. It seemed that people who barely knew the students were making major decisions for them.

Parents vs. the School Board

The Robisons reported in their 1991 article for *Exceptional Parent* that they spent the summer going over the law. They felt it was important for Lynn to remain where she was. The Robisons called the Department of Education to find out why Lynn and other students like her were being moved. Members of the board of education and administrators told them that Lynn's new school would have better building access, more resources, and teachers trained to meet her specific needs. The Robisons felt that Lynn was thriving where she was. They did not want her moved. They read up on the law so they would be prepared when the time came. Finally, the school district met with the parents. They said that parents had no choice. Students would either go to the new school voluntarily, or they would be sent there once the staff had been hired.

The Robisons and the other parents were prepared to fight. They had the law on their side. IDEA stated that each child would go to the school he or she would normally attend if the student was not disabled. If the child's education plan required a different facility, only then would he or she have to be moved to a different school. Lynn had done well at school. She had made friends. All the other kids had similar experiences. The parents talked to the board about how well their children were doing in school. They talked about the friends they had made. They quoted the law, which stated that the parents and the staff should determine where each student would go to school. The school board could not make those decisions for them.

When the school year began, Lynn was in her regular third-grade classroom with her friends. Parents of the general education students seemed confused. They had been told that Lynn and other students with disabilities were being moved. The struggle between the parents and the school board continued. The parents met with the school board. They brought information that showed how integration helped all students, regardless of their abilities. They talked about their relationship with the schools. It had been excellent at one time, and now that communication was lost. Teachers seemed under pressure to agree that some students should be moved. To the Robisons, it seemed as though some teachers were afraid they would lose their jobs if they disagreed with the school board.

The school board pressed on with its plan. Tyler, another special-needs student, was tested over the course of three days. Both his family and the school board had lawyers representing them. The tests showed that Tyler could stay, but the school board wanted him out. For four years, Tyler's parents and the school board had court cases, but in the end, the

CAMPING OUT

When Brian Einwag was diagnosed with spondylitis, a type of arthritis that attacks the spine, he and his wife, Muffet, met many special-needs children who were very restricted. They decided to start a camp for them so that they could enjoy the same kind of summer camp experience that many other kids had. Camp Florida Fishtales is a one-week camp where kids go fishing, do arts and crafts, go on nature walks, and sing around a campfire. Each child is paired with a camp counselor. The grounds are wheelchair accessible so that everyone has access to every activity. Even though Brian passed away because of his disease in 2001, the camp is still active.

school board backed down. Anne Robison felt it was because they did not want to pay four years of Tyler's legal fees.

As Lynn grew older, she became more aware of the difficulty special-needs students had going to regular schools. She once wrote a response to everything that was going on, saying, "People are just people," and "if we don't go to regular schools, how will we ever get a job?"

SPECIAL EDUCATION VS. GENERAL EDUCATION

More recent examples have shown that students with disabilities can do well in mainstream classrooms. The point has been proven to some parents in New York City's P.S. 75. Jed, a student with a learning disability, was having difficulty in his $20,000-per-year private school. He often got into trouble for kicking and sometimes biting others. When he started kindergarten, he was already a reader. Yet, at the end of third grade, he was still reading the same books that he was in kindergarten. His mother, Sarah, decided to enroll him in P.S. 75 on the Upper West Side. His new class of 31 students had nine special-education students, including himself. Jed did not even know who they were.

In Jed's new classroom, work was individualized. Students read books on many levels at the same time. There were two teachers in the room. One was a special-education teacher, but the other was not. Both teachers circulated the room and helped all the students, regardless of their needs. This model is called "collaborative team teaching." When it is done well, students do well, and there is usually no need to separate them in different facilities. One teacher of a self-contained class with learning- and emotionally disabled students found that students who were in general-education classes performed better and had better behavior.

Still, opposition to these blended classrooms continues. Some parents do not want students with disabilities in their kids' classrooms. Some classes are not well managed. Some classes become a dumping ground for struggling students. Teachers agree that the model can work. It needs good teachers and support from parents and school administrators.

5 WOMEN AND POLITICS

"Somewhere out in this audience may even be someone who will one day follow in my footsteps, and preside over the White House as the president's spouse. I wish him well!"

—Barbara Bush (1925–), former First Lady,
at a Wellesley College commencement

For centuries, women were not viewed as being equal to men. Men owned the land. Men held positions of power in government. Men made the decisions. In some places, women inflicted physical injuries on themselves for the sake of beauty. But by the nineteenth century, women all over the world were trying to find an equal place.

WOMEN AS EQUALS

In 1892, in their very first issue, the women's press in Egypt expressed concern about the way women were treated and viewed by society. Oddly enough, their complaints went unheard until a man, Qasim Amin, wrote *Women's Liberation* in 1899. At the time, girls were the property of their father, and wives were the property of their husband. Women were not allowed to be educated. Amin felt that this treatment was the same as slavery. He thought that girls and women should be allowed to go to school.

About the same time in China, there was a movement to end foot-binding. At the time, small feet were thought to be a sign of beauty. As a result, young girls had their feet bound in tight bandages to prevent growth. Their feet developed high arches, and they were unable to walk well. The process was painful. Many women lost their toes and got infections because of the process of binding. After the fall of the last dynasty in China, the government of the New Republic of China officially banned the practice. With women's feet reforming, the women's movement began to take shape.

Though making headway in other countries, the women's movement in Britain was not gaining much ground in the 1800s. A British mother-and-daughter team, Emmeline Pankhurst and her daughter Christabel, decided to take more action for their cause. The group put out a monthly newspaper called *Votes for Women*. They began to protest the government. One of their protests was "no vote, no tax." The women felt that if they were not allowed to vote, they should not have to pay taxes. Members of the group were arrested and put in jail. While there, they continued their protests by refusing to eat. From the British women's movement came the word *suffragette*. The word *suffrage* means "the right to vote." The suffragettes were women seeking the right to vote for all women.

In the United States, there was at least one group of women who were treated equally with their male peers. Quakers believed that women should be well educated and have as much say in politics as men. In fact, they believed that all people were equal. In the 1800s, slavery was still a part of the American economy. Lucretia Mott and her husband, James, were Quakers who felt that slavery was evil. They often hid runaway slaves in their home.

Mott traveled to England to participate in the Anti-Slavery Convention. Even though she was an official delegate, she was not allowed to sit or even be seen by the men who were attending the convention. Another American woman who

One of America's earliest feminists and reformers, Lucretia Mott was a Quaker preacher dedicated to achieving equality for all of America's disadvantaged, including Native Americans, women, slaves, and free African Americans.

was sitting in a roped-off women's-only section protested that she could not see Mott when it was Mott's turn to speak. She was also upset that women had to sit in a separate section. This woman was Elizabeth Cady Stanton.

Stanton was the daughter of a lawyer. From a young age, she liked to read her father's law books and debate legal issues. Stanton began to notice how the law disfavored women, especially married ones. Unlike many other girls at the time, Stanton was well educated. She went to a school where she outperformed many of the boys in her class. Yet, after graduation, the boys were able to go on to college, while Stanton was left out because she was a girl. Her interest in law and education, as well as her frustration with the double standard for women, fueled her belief in equality. That led her to the Anti-Slavery Convention in England while she was on her honeymoon.

Stanton and her new husband were both in favor of ending slavery. Unlike her husband, Stanton was also in favor of women's rights. In her marriage vows, she refused to say she would "obey," which was a common vow for marrying women to take. She and Mott were very much alike, so when they met at the Anti-Slavery Convention, they instantly became friends. They decided that they would hold a women's movement convention in the United States as soon as they both returned there.

WHO SHOULD VOTE?

Back in the United States, Mott and Stanton organized the Women's Rights Convention in Seneca Falls, New York. At the 1848 convention, women signed a declaration that was modeled after the Declaration of Independence. It was called the Declaration of Sentiments. It stated, "All men and women were created equal." It asked that all the people who signed the document would work to right the wrongs that women suffered. The convention's primary goal was to get women the ability to vote.

Elizabeth Cady Stanton was an American reformer and leader in the women's rights movement. She helped organize the first event demanding women's suffrage in the United States—the 1848 Women's Rights Convention in Seneca Falls, New York.

In an 1860 speech, Stanton said, "The prejudice against color, of which we hear so much, is no stronger than that against sex. It is produced by the same cause and manifested very much in the same way." When the Civil War ended in 1865 and African Americans wanted to have the Fourteenth and Fifteenth Amendments to the Constitution ratified, Stanton opposed the measures. The Fourteenth Amendment would define African Americans as citizens of the United States and guarantee them rights and protection as citizens under the law. The Fifteenth Amendment would give African Americans the right to vote. Although Stanton was an abolitionist, she did not want these amendments to pass as they were worded. She believed that the language of the new laws should include women. She had been a friend of Frederick Douglass, a famous former slave who fought for abolition and the rights of African Americans. Now they stood on opposite sides.

Douglass believed that white women had a voice in the voting process because their husbands and fathers had the right to vote. Stanton felt that African-American men already had the right to vote because all men were able to vote according to the Constitution; her real goal was to get all women to vote. To get others to see value in having women vote and to argue against the political idea that women may not have been educated enough to vote, Stanton stated that she was in favor of "educated suffrage," wherein all people would take tests to prove that they were educated enough to vote. Although it may not have been Stanton's intention, this idea would have left uneducated freed slaves out of the voting process. Many people believe that her actions split up the effort to give African Americans and women the rights they wanted. Her friend Lucretia Mott believed in both causes. She found herself refereeing arguments between Stanton and others. Some women in Stanton's organization, the National Woman Suffrage Association, did not like her stand against

(continues on page 76)

WOMEN IN THE LEAD

While women all over the world have had to struggle for equal ground with men, these extraordinary women have made it to the highest positions in their countries.

Sirimavo Bandaranaike was the prime minister of Sri Lanka on three different occasions. Her husband was prime minister before her. When he was assassinated, she took over leadership of the political party he had formed. The election in 1960 made her the first female world leader. Bandaranaike was reelected in 1970 and stayed in power until 1977, then was in power again from 1994 to 2000. Bandaranaike died on October 10, 2000. It was Election Day, and she had already cast her vote.

Indira Priyadarshini Gandhi was born on November 19, 1917, to the Nehru family. Politics was the Nehru family's business. Her grandfather was a nationalist leader. Her father became the first prime minister after India gained its independence from Britain. When her father died in 1964, the new prime minister, Lal Bahadur Shastri, appointed her as a minister. When Shastri died in 1965, Gandhi took his place. She became prime minister in 1966 and served until 1977. She became prime minister again in 1980 and served until her assassination in 1984.

Golda Meir was born on May 3, 1898, in what is now Ukraine. Her family moved to Milwaukee, Wisconsin, when she was a child. Although she did not know any English when she began school, she was the class valedictorian when she graduated. She married at age 19 and moved to Israel. Meir quickly became involved in politics. She was one of the 24 people who signed the Israeli Declaration of Independence on May 14, 1948. After a long career in politics, Meir retired in 1966 when she was diagnosed with lymphoma, a type of cancer. Yet, she continued to work for the prime minister, Levi Eshkol. When Eshkol died suddenly in 1969, Meir was elected as party leader. She was the first woman to hold the post of prime minister in Israel. She served until 1974, when she resigned.

Margaret Thatcher had a long tenure as prime minister of the United Kingdom. She was first elected in 1979 and served until 1990. Before

Sirimavo Ratwatte Bandaranaike *(left)* became the first female world leader in 1960 when she became prime minister of Sri Lanka after her husband, then the prime minister, died. Her daughter, Chandrika Bandaranaike Kumaratunga *(right)*, became president of Sri Lanka in 1994. The two are pictured in 1964 at a London airport.

she became prime minister, she was elected as leader of the Conservative Party beginning in 1975. She was the first, and so far the only, woman to hold either title. Thatcher was used to getting attention in the media. When she began her political career, she was the youngest woman in the Conservative Party. Some have said that Thatcher only needed four hours of sleep a night during her time as prime minister. She was called the "Iron Lady" for her tough stand against communism.

(continued from page 73)

the amendments. They split off and formed their own organization called the American Woman Suffrage Association.

Stanton befriended another famous African American—Sojourner Truth, a former slave and a feminist. Yet, Stanton felt strongly that women should be given the right to vote at the same time as African Americans. After the Fifteenth Amendment was passed giving African Americans the right to vote, her previous argument that voters should be educated created a backlash. By the 1880s, some Southern states had difficult voter qualification laws. African Americans had to prove they could read and write before they were allowed to vote. Without access to schools, many were unable to cast their votes. Plus, some states had a special tax for voters who wanted to cast their vote. A "grandfather clause" in the tax eliminated it for those whose grandfathers were able to vote. This meant that whites could continue voting free of charge, but most African Americans could not. The poll tax was not eliminated until the Twenty-fourth Amendment to the Constitution passed in 1964.

Stanton did not live to see women get the vote. Another woman from a Quaker background would get them there.

GOING TO WASHINGTON

Alice Paul was born in New Jersey. As a Quaker, she was well educated. She graduated first in her class in high school, and then went on to get several degrees from universities in the United States and England, including a master's degree in social work, a doctorate, and two law degrees. She was inspired to join the suffrage movement when she heard famous suffragette Christabel Pankhurst speak in England.

When she returned to the United States, Paul tried to continue in the footsteps of Elizabeth Stanton. She lobbied Congress to make an amendment to the Constitution. She found that the suffragette effort was not working. While other

American suffragette Alice Paul, seen here in 1912, helped form the National Woman's Party and fought for the suffrage movement. She wrote the first draft of the Equal Rights Amendment.

suffragettes decided to work on a state-by-state basis, Paul felt it was time for a radical change. She and a few others formed their own party, the National Woman's Party (NWP). They decided to employ some of the tactics they had learned from the English suffragettes.

Paul decided to approach Congress again to amend the Constitution. She organized protests, mass meetings, picket lines, and hunger strikes. In January 1917, the NWP picketed the White House. World War I was in full swing. People were outraged that the NWP picketed the president at a time of war. However, there was no reason to stop them from picketing because it was not against the law. Finally, just to get them out of the way, some of them, including Paul, were arrested for obstructing traffic. A year later, President Woodrow Wilson asked Congress to give women the right to vote. Congress held back on the discussion. Women were finally given the vote in 1920, three years after they picketed the White House.

Paul felt that the right to vote did not mean that women were seen as equal to men. To fix this, she wrote the Equal Rights Amendment (ERA). It would guarantee equal pay, equal consideration for jobs, and equal protection under the law for women and men. From 1920 to today, the ERA has never passed in Congress. There have been other laws passed that guarantee certain rights for women, such as Title IX and the Equal Pay Act.

Title IX was a 1972 amendment to the Constitution that affected education. It states, "No person in the United States shall, on the basis of sex, be excluded from participation in, be denied the benefits of, or be subjected to discrimination under any education program or activity receiving Federal financial assistance." Although the original intention was to cover educational programs, it has most affected women's sports at the high school and college level. The ability for women to have great athletic programs that were formerly only available to men has paved the way for women's professional sports teams. For example, the 2004 U.S. Women's

HABIBA SARABI

All over the world, women have gotten the right to vote. They have made their way into politics. They lead countries and organizations and businesses. In some small pockets of the world, however, they still do not have the same rights as men. Afghanistan is one of those places. Yet, in the province of Bamiyan, one woman has risen to make a difference.

Habiba Sarabi's political streak showed itself when she was at Kabul University in the 1980s. She organized demonstrations against the Soviet occupation of her country. After university, she became a pharmacist, a wife, and a mother. Then the Taliban took over Afghanistan, and she fled with her children to Pakistan.

(continues)

Habiba Sarabi started a secret school for girls in her home country of Afghanistan at a time when women were not allowed to be educated under the Taliban. A year after the Taliban fell from power in 2001, she was named as the country's minister for women's affairs. In 2005, she became governor of the province of Bamiyan. She was the first woman to be named governor of any Afghan province.

(continued)

Sarabi found a job training teachers in Pakistan, but she wanted to help in her own country. The Taliban did not allow girls to be educated. A 2005 *USA Today* article reported that 86 percent of women and girls over age 15 could not read or write. The Taliban also did not provide health care for women and girls. Many women have died in childbirth. Eighty-seven percent of those deaths were preventable, according to the same *USA Today* article. A pregnant woman had to ask her husband's permission to visit the doctor each month for a checkup. Sarabi snuck back into Afghanistan and began a secret girls' school. When the Taliban fell in 2001, Sarabi returned home. She was named minister for women's affairs the following year. Then in 2005, she was named the governor of Bamiyan, an Afghan province. She was the first woman in that role.

The people of Bamiyan province are considered to follow a more moderate brand of Islam. Women are more likely to vote, and men are more likely to consider a female candidate than in other parts of the country. Sarabi is a role model to other women in the country who have entered politics. They all face strong opposition by men who still believe that women should stay at home. Some female candidates find it hard to get everyone to understand that women are equally capable.

Even though some women are being accepted into politics, they still face the same kind of stereotypes that normal women do. One storeowner has a poster of a candidate on his wall. He insists that he will only vote for the most beautiful. Even Sarabi, who now runs a province and fights back against warlords who threaten the people and stop much-needed progress, is criticized based on her looks. According to one election officer, everybody likes the job she is doing. The only complaint he has heard is that "she's put on a little weight since she took office."

National Soccer Team won gold in the Olympics. The WNBA (Women's National Basketball Association) was formed in 1996, 50 years after male ballplayers had the same opportunity with the NBA.

Equality in education has not been the only move forward. In 1963, when the Equal Pay Act was put in effect, women earned only 58 cents for every dollar that a man earned. Even with this act of Congress, women who have the same education and experience as men still earn less. In 2005, women earned 77 cents for every dollar that a man earned. That number decreases for minorities. African-American women earn 69 cents to every dollar a white man earns, and Hispanic women earn 59 cents per dollar. Over a lifetime, that amounts to a difference of hundreds of thousands of dollars.

The WAGE Project (Women Are Getting Even) is led by Evelyn F. Murphy, the author of *Getting Even: Why Women*

The WNBA's Sheryl Swoopes, Rebecca Lobo, and Lisa Leslie—Olympic gold medalists for the United States—hold basketballs designating the new WNBA teams to which they were assigned in 1997, the year after the WNBA was formed.

Don't Get Paid Like Men and What to Do About It. Murphy, the former lieutenant governor of Massachusetts, aims to get women on an even pay scale with men. As much advancement as the women's movement has made, many feel that equality is still missing.

COMING TO AMERICA

6

"Remember, remember always, that all of us, and you and I especially, are descended from immigrants and revolutionists."

—*Franklin D. Roosevelt (1882–1945), former U.S. president*

Immigrants have been coming to America since the 1600s to seek a better life. Every day, the United States Immigration and Naturalization Service receives applications from people wanting to become American citizens. Many of these people are from non-English-speaking countries, and one of the many barriers to becoming part of the American community is learning the language. The other part is becoming educated and finding a job. The biggest source of immigration to the United States is south of the border in Mexico. Mexican immigrants have been a source of labor for decades, but they are still integrating into American society. Mexican immigrants face a triple form of prejudice. They are judged based on the color of their skin, their ability to speak English, and their economic standing.

MIGRANT WORKERS

Cesar Chavez came from a Mexican family. His grandfather was a hard worker who moved with his wife and children to the United States and began a farm. The entire Chavez family worked on the farm and in the store that they owned. Eventually, all of Cesar Chavez's uncles and aunts moved away to places of their own, but Chavez's father stayed to run the store. When the economic depression hit in the 1920s, money was tight for everyone, and the Chavez family lost its home. They became migrant farmworkers. It was the hardest kind of life they had ever experienced.

Migrant farmworkers move from farm to farm, helping out with any crop that is in season. They plant, weed, grow, and pick a crop, but they must continually move to where the work is. Children of migrant workers often are not in any one school for a long time, so their education is patchy. Because they are unable to stay at one school, it can be difficult to learn, so many of these children fall behind in schoolwork. Cesar Chavez was one of these children. It was not for lack of brains, only lack of a continuous education. By the time Chavez was 15 years old, he had completed school only up to the seventh grade. He had to drop out to help his family work.

Despite the constant moving, Chavez's mother made sure that he had a good upbringing. She was Catholic and raised him to be religious. She also taught him to always help the poor and never to fight. "It takes two to fight," she would say. "One cannot do it alone." His father believed in supporting his fellow workers. If one worker was cheated and walked off the job, the Chavez family would follow them, too. Chavez's father also belonged to farmworkers' unions, which tried to find a better way of life for the migrant worker.

As a young man, Chavez met a priest named Father McDonnell who came to give Mass to the migrant workers where they lived in Sal Si Puedes, California. In Spanish, Sal Si Puedes means "escape if you can." McDonnell befriended Chavez and taught him about St. Francis of Assisi, who lived in service of people who were poor. He also taught him about Mohandas Gandhi, who led the people of India to independence without using violence. These great people echoed the values that Chavez's mother had taught him, and that would help him later on as a leader for the migrant worker. Father McDonnell also taught Chavez something that was perhaps more important. He taught him about the economics of the average migrant worker's situation. He had pictures of the shacks that the migrant workers had to live in. Sometimes entire families of 12 or more people would live in one-room houses that were no better than tents. In the winter, there was no heat and no insulation against the cold air. Chavez himself knew about these conditions. One winter, his family had no place to live. He and his brothers had to sleep outside in the cold. His shoes disintegrated because of the damp air, and when he was able to go to school, he had to walk through the mud barefoot. Then the priest showed Chavez pictures of a farm owner's mansion and migrant workers' labor camps. The camps, which provided temporary and very poor shelter to workers, paled in comparison to the farm owner's home.

GETTING ORGANIZED

Chavez wanted to help migrant workers find better wages and better working conditions. A few years later, a man who worked for the government came looking for Chavez. He talked to Chavez about the stream that ran behind Sal Si Puedes and how it was dirty from factory waste. The children of the migrant families played in that stream and often became sick. This man wanted to help Chavez and the others. He told Chavez that everyone needed to vote. If they could pick a candidate who would help them, then they would have a better chance to change their fate.

Chavez immediately went to work getting Mexican Americans registered to vote. Yet, when they went out to the voting booths, some of the deputy registrars gave the new voters a hard time. They asked them if they were really Americans. They asked them to prove that they could read and write.

Many of the Mexican Americans went home from the polls without voting. The Mexican Americans were more likely to vote for the Democratic candidates because those candidates supported the issues of the poor. Most of the registrars were Republican.

Chavez signed a formal complaint about what had happened. He did not care what the newly elected officials did to him. This action gained him a lot of respect. He then left his farmwork and began working for the Community Service Organization (CSO). His job was to organize migrant workers and educate them about what they could do to help themselves. While there, he tried to create a farmworkers' union, but the CSO did not want that. The most powerful labor organization in the United States—the AFL-CIO (American Federation of Labor and Congress of Industrial Organizations)—had a union for farmworkers called the Agricultural Workers Organizing Committee (AWOC). Chavez did not want to join them. At the time, he felt that he needed more freedom than the large union would give him. He also felt that if the AFL-CIO were feeding the smaller union money, it would want to tell the union how to spend the money. Instead, Chavez began his own union, the National Farm Workers Association, or NFWA.

Chavez drove with his youngest child from farm to farm, talking to workers. He needed them to join the union so that they could have a united front. He understood their circumstances. He went with them to doctor's appointments, helped them write letters, helped them to translate—anything they needed. They knew he was there to help, and he won them over. The migrant laborers worked under grim conditions. When they weeded lettuce, they had to use a short-handled hoe. The lettuce was delicate and the hoe forced them to work close to the ground so that they could thin-out the plants without damaging them. The consequence of this meant they had to work all day bent to the ground. When they planted onions, they pushed into the ground with their fingers and then pushed the plants in. This work also kept them hunched over for hours and hours. The heat was unbearable, often over 100°F. Many workers wore masks over their faces to protect them against the dust and the insects that hovered close to the ground. Some wore handkerchiefs to keep the sweat from falling into their eyes. The farm owners provided water but sometimes charged the laborers to drink it. Often there was no toilet in the fields that the workers could use. Plus, the pesticides that the growers used on their crops were

Cesar Chavez led the Delano grape pickers' strike, bringing strikers and sympathizers on a 300-mile, 25-day pilgrimage from Delano, CA, to Sacramento in an attempt to meet with Governor Edmund G. ("Pat") Brown on Easter Sunday in 1966. Above, Chavez waves to the crowd from the steps of the California State Capitol, after a settlement was reached with the grape producer Schenley Industries.

poisoning the workers. Still, most migrant workers only made about $1,500 per year. At the time, the federal poverty level was $3,000. It was hardly enough to survive.

Of all the farm laborers, grape pickers were the most fortunate. Grape farming took up 10 months of the year, and so it provided a steadier stream of work. Grape farm laborers did not need to move around the way other laborers did, but Chavez and the unions thought it was important to get them to join the unions. The laborers were not just Mexican American. Some were Filipino, and some were Indian. Farm owners pitted them against each other by race. If they were fighting each other, they would never come together to fight the owners. Chavez stopped that.

In 1965, the AFL-CIO decided to strike against the Delano grape farms. The workers were mainly Filipino, but Chavez and the Mexican-American workers of his union decided to join them. They all walked off the farms and marched from town to town. They explained what they were doing and told people to boycott the farms by not eating the grapes. Chavez made sure that everyone knew that they were not to fight. The strike benefited not just the migrant workers in California but farmworkers everywhere. The plight of the workers was televised. Across America, people saw how the oranges they got from Florida were picked. Even the pineapple pickers in Hawaii were able to negotiate a better contract. People were boycotting grapes across America. Dockworkers in Britain who knew about the strike refused to offload California grapes to support the strikers. The farm owners were losing a lot of money. Finally, on Easter Sunday in 1966, the march reached its end. Chavez was able to announce that he had signed a deal with one of the farm owners to recognize the union. Workers were to get an immediate pay raise. However, other farm owners did not recognize the union so easily.

The growers were losing money as more and more people decided not to buy California grapes, so they became devious. They used labels bought from other grape farms. They invented new labels so that stores would buy them. When the unions learned of this, they told people to only buy grapes that had the union label on it: the black eagle that was on Chavez's union flag. Eventually, every grape grower was calling the union to find out what they had to do to get the eagle on their boxes. It was a triumph for Chavez and a blow to economic prejudice.

NEW IMMIGRANTS IN OLD CITIES

Immigrants are now moving farther away from the usual border cities to find work. In Siler City, North Carolina, immigrants come for jobs at the local poultry plants. Some are Korean, others are Mexican, but they all are working for little money and are doing very difficult work. They pluck, cut, debone, and gut the chickens. In a 2000 article for Salon. com, titled "When David Duke Goes Marching In," one worker reported he had been working there for four years making $7.40 an hour. That year, he got a 10-cent raise. He called the work hard, cold, and tough on the body. Because the work is difficult, workers leave often and need to be replaced. The same article reported that owners might prefer illegal workers because they can be easily replaced if they join together to demand better wages and better conditions.

Still, complaints about the immigrants continue. The arguments are many and varied. One of the arguments involves the impact of non-English-speaking immigrants on the school system. Many immigrant students do not speak English fluently. Some American parents think that teachers will spend a lot of time helping students who do not understand the language and not enough time teaching other students new skills. In Siler City, the test scores have in fact been lowered because of these issues, and many white families have moved to mostly white school districts where they feel their children will get a better education. Unfortunately, their actions sometimes help to further lower the average of test scores in the schools that they leave.

Others are concerned that the value of their home will go down when immigrants move into the area. In fact, the influx of more families has helped the housing market. In mid-1990, a small house cost about $39,000. By the turn of the millennium, the same type of house had increased in value to about $59,000, according to the National Association of Home Builders.

Some are concerned that their tax dollars are being used to try to help immigrants integrate into American society. They feel that their taxes should be spent on educating their children and on other much-needed services in the city. However, many immigrants, even illegal ones, pay taxes too.

In 2000, some residents of Siler City who did not want illegal immigrants in their town organized a rally. They invited David Duke, a former leader of the Ku Klux Klan (KKK),

PLAYING SOCCER

Paul Cuadros is a freelance writer. He was born in Peru and is now an immigrant living in the United States. In 1999, he came to Siler City, North Carolina, following a story about immigrants integrating into American society. He covered the 2000 rally at which David Duke spoke. He saw division everywhere, even in the schools. He wanted to do something about it. Cuadros went to the principal of Jordan-Matthews High School in Siler City and asked to start a soccer team with him as the coach. The principal was against the idea at first. Cuadros listened to all of the obstacles to forming a team, and he responded to each one. He informed parents, found sponsors who would pay for the team's uniforms and equipment, and located a place for the team to play. No one was sure the team would work out, even the players. Yet, when the players saw their new blue-and-white Jets uniforms, they began to feel like they belonged to something.

At their first games, the mostly Hispanic team suffered from harsh words coming from the stands. The coach helped them to respond to the rally. The KKK is a group for American-born, white Christians. It is anti-minority, anti-Catholic, anti-Semitic, and even against other whites who are not of English-German or Protestant backgrounds. Duke argued that companies hire illegal laborers instead of American citizens because they can pay them less money. He told the people who attended the rally that they were being "plucked" just like the chickens at the poultry processing plants. At a victory lunch later that day, Duke was seen to be eating chicken. Paul Cuadros, the reporter who wrote "When David Duke Goes Marching In," wondered if Duke thought about where his chicken had come from.

In a 2006 report for National Public Radio, reporter Jennifer Ludden found a former anti-immigration supporter who had changed his mind. Rick Givens once agreed with Duke.

by getting better scores. The players wanted to embarrass the other teams so that their prejudiced words would mean nothing. As the Jets began to win, people started to like them. In a *New York Times* interview in 2004, Cuadros stated, "It's hard not to like a winner." Their success reflected on the whole school, not just on the Hispanics who attended the school. By the time the team rose up the ranks to win the championship game, they were embraced by the community as a whole.

They were still unsure how people felt about them as they marched in the Siler City Christmas parade in December 2004. Some of them walked with their heads down. Yet, when they heard the cheers of the crowd, they became encouraged. As they walked through the same downtown area where the former KKK leader held the anti-immigration rally, the soccer team was thrilled at the support from the crowd. They picked up their heads. They warmed up to the crowd. It was a big change from four years before.

THE CENTER FOR NEW NORTH CAROLINIANS

Jaimie Foster works with immigrant families who have children up to three years old. When asked how important it is to have cultural brokers, or people who help immigrants integrate into a new culture, Foster gives a background story that could describe some of her clients. She asks you to imagine a family living in a small town in Mexico. There are three children, and they are all crying from hunger. The family is too poor to feed them. The mother and father decide to pack up and move to the United States. The family walks across the hot desert for three days. Then they hop on a bus and get into the United States. From there, they need to find a small town to start a new life. They need to find a place to stay. The father has to find work immediately. The mother has to stay home to take care of the kids. They may need to find a doctor. The older children have to get into school. The family does not know how anything works, and they do not speak the language. The parents worry constantly about deportation, about making enough money, and about the way people think of them. They may become depressed, and that depression begins to affect the kids.

Fortunately for immigrants who move to North Carolina, the Center for New North Carolinians at the University of North Carolina is there to help. Foster does everything from finding pregnant moms low-cost prenatal care to finding a family dentist. The center also helps parents fill out application forms to get their children into preschool and helps them to understand that children must be in school full-time beginning at age five.

"It's like someone took you and dropped you off in a small town in Japan," Foster says. "Then they say, 'go live your life.'" It is a difficult prospect.

Foster understands how crucial the newborn to three-year-old age group is. Children who do not know their alphabet and numbers by the time they are in kindergarten are already behind. Foster helps the parents and the kids get the support they need so that they are prepared when school begins. Of the people that Foster works with, only a few have been in North Carolina for more than five years. Most of them are recent arrivals, some as recent as two months. Unfortunately, the center is not able to help everyone. Foster says she tries not to turn anyone away, but she sometimes has to refer people to other places where they can find help.

As chairman of the Chatham County, North Carolina, Board of Commissioners, Givens sent a letter to the U.S. Immigration and Naturalization Service asking for help to find a way to send illegal workers back to their own country. He complained that tax money was being used to help illegal immigrants when it was needed to do other things for the citizens of Siler City. Some Hispanic parents feared that they would be deported, and so they pulled their children out of the public schools. They hoped to stay out of the public eye. Then Givens decided to go on a fact-finding mission to Mexico. The trip was funded by the University of North Carolina. The university has a division devoted to helping immigrants settle in the United States. The weeklong trip changed Givens. He saw schools that had few supplies, including books. He met students who were struggling to attend school because of the cost. He gave $500 to one student who was disabled and could no longer attend school. Givens also promised to stock the library of another school. When he returned, he expressed that people needed to concentrate more on finding ways to help immigrants integrate into American life.

In 2006, six years after the anti-immigration rally, there was a pro-immigration rally in Siler City. About 4,000 people came to show their support for the nearly 11 million illegal immigrants then living in the United States. They waved flags and had signs that read "I pay taxes" and "Thank you, Siler City, we love you." During the peaceful rally, The Chatham News reported that Ilana Dubester of the *Hispanic Liaison* told the crowd, "No human being is illegal. We are your neighbors. We are your spouses. We are your fellow church members. We are working hard and paying our share of taxes." The protesters wanted lawmakers to help illegal immigrants settle legally in the United States.

In the meantime, new calls to secure the U.S.-Mexico border have been made. This initiative falls under the umbrella of the Department of Homeland Security. However, there has been no aggression from south of the border. U.S. politicians now work hard to get Hispanic votes, and companies rec-ognize the buying power of immigrants. In Siler City, a new Wal-Mart has been built to accommodate the immigrants who moved to the area. The store counts on the immigrants to buy its products.

IMAGE IS EVERYTHING

"Beauty is in the eye of the beholder."

—proverb

Some prejudices are so much a part of our society that they are integrated into everyday images. Television, newspapers, and magazines bombard viewers and readers with images daily. Many may not realize that the majority of the people behind American mass media—the writers—are from the dominant group in our society: white males.

IMAGE AND MEDIA

A 2007 report by the Writers Guild of America reported that, even though 30 percent of the American population is non-white, only 10 percent of television writers are from minority groups. In the film industry, that number drops to 6 percent. Writers' pay is also unequal. White writers continue to make considerably more. In 2005, a white television writer made $97,956, while minority writers made an average of $78,107. In the film industry, the number was closer, at $77,537 for white writers and $66,666 for minorities. Another report found that minorities also play smaller roles on-screen. In 2007, 58 percent of characters were male, 77 percent were white, 12 percent were African American, 6 percent were Hispanic, and

3 percent were Asian. Of the remaining characters, 4 percent were multiracial, 1 percent were Middle Eastern, and 1 percent were Native Alaskan.

Even in the news, minorities seem to get more coverage in connection with crime. A 1991 study by Canadian Charles Ungerleider found that some news reporters are basically telling stories. They cast the people in those stories as heroes, villains, or victims. Among those routinely cast as villains are minorities. Although in Canada immigrants are less likely to break the law than native-born Canadians, 54 percent of all articles in a four-month period reported immigrants involved in criminal activities. Some experts feel that this kind of reporting is damaging both to the immigrant communities and to the public as a whole.

VIDEO GAMES

Minority bias is not only limited to television. A 2001 study by the organization Children Now found that video games in the United States represented a significant amount of bias. The study, titled "Fair Play? Violence, Gender and Race in Video Games," found that 86 percent of the main characters in video games were white males. Seventy percent of Asian male characters were fighters. Eighty percent of African-American males were sports competitors. Nearly 90 percent of African-American females were victims of violence. That was twice the number of white female victims. Researchers also found that 79 percent of African-American males were portrayed as verbally and physically aggressive. Only 57 percent of white males were characterized in that way.

The same group did a study in 1988 that showed that children associate white characters with having lots of money, a good education, leadership, success in school, and intelligence. On the other hand, they associate minority characters with breaking the law, having no money, being lazy, and having bad behavior.

Stereotyping is not only about crime. Immigrants and minorities get more coverage in news about sports and entertainment, and less in politics and business. A study by Professor Robert Entman and Harvard students Debra Burns Melican and Irma Munoz found that "experts" called upon to discuss topics are mainly white males. If minority experts are used, it is usually in response to stories that involve their specific minority group. That study was reported in the book, *The Black Image in the White Mind* (2000), by Entman and fellow Harvard professor Andrew Rojecki. Jeff Cohen, founder of Fairness and Accuracy in Media (FAIR), found similar results in that organization's early 1990's study.

A 2000 article in *Jet* magazine titled "Black Characters Segregated on TV Shows, Report Finds" indicated that only a few emerging television stations had shows with African-American characters in main roles. Of those shows, African Americans were mainly in comedic and not dramatic roles. The *Jet* article also found that the WB station, later renamed CW, had the most diverse shows and that the Fox network had the least. Even when minority characters are being included on the major networks, such as Fox and NBC, the minorities often play small roles.

Media producers argued for years that the lack of diversity on television was about money, not racism. Specifically, they were talking about advertising money. The Media Awareness Network published the following findings in a 2008 article titled, "The Economics of Ethnic and Racial Stereotyping." At the height of the black television shows *The Jamie Foxx Show* and *The Steve Harvey Show*, a 30-second commercial cost less than one aired during *Felicity*, a show in which the main characters are white. However, all three shows had about the same number of viewers for their first-run episodes. *The Steve Harvey Show* had 500,000 more viewers than the all-white *Dawson's Creek*, but a 30-second commercial brought in $63,000 more for *Dawson's Creek*. As a result of these findings, the 1990s saw a change in the way advertisers looked at different TV shows. And viewers became more likely to see racial diversity in commercials for all kinds of products nationwide.

SIZE BIAS:
THE LAST ACCEPTABLE PREJUDICE?

In 2007, Karen Chambers and Susan Alexander, reporting for *Education Magazine*, did research about how media affects the self-image of women in college. The study was called "Project Innovation Summer 2007." They gathered 75 female students from ages 18 to 21. The students were assigned to three groups. The first group watched a program titled "Slim Hopes," which was about body image depicted in various media. The second group read an article by the same person who did the video. The article was on the same subject and used many of the same images. The third group was a control group and asked to complete a maze. The researchers found that the students who had watched the video said that their bodies were close to their "ideal" body image. Researchers also found that the groups who watched the video or read the article were both able to answer informed questions about women and body image.

A similar study reported in a *Washington Post* article in 2002 titled, "Goodbye to Girlhood," was done on the self-image of seventh-grade girls. The girls were shown pictures of women in magazines. Afterward, they reported a drop in their own satisfaction with their bodies and a rise in depression. The report concluded that advertisers rely on this reaction. People who are happy with their looks do not buy beauty products.

Boys are not immune either. In 2003, CBS News interviewed a teenager who had been pursuing his ideal body image by using steroids. Anabolic steroids are a synthetic version of the male hormone testosterone. The hormone helps the body to build muscle. However, there are serious risks involved in taking steroids, including liver damage, premature heart attacks or strokes, high cholesterol, weak tendons, depression, and irritability. "So many people, especially teenagers, feel self-conscious about their bodies, and if it bothers you that much, you're willing to go to any extreme to change that," the anonymous teen said. He was working out seven days a week. When he still was not getting the results he wanted, he began to take steroids. "People would go, 'Wow, look at you, you're the picture of health,'" he said. Yet, behind the scenes, he was anything but healthy. His hair was falling out. He would wake up angry and get angrier as the day progressed. In 2002, nearly half a million teenage boys were using steroids. A Harvard University-funded study showed that the majority of teen boys who use steroids do it for their looks, not just because they are athletes. The researchers found that boys as young as age 11 preferred more buff body types—body types that were impossible to get without the use of steroids.

In the TLC documentary *The Man Whose Arms Exploded*, a researcher looked at action figures from the 1970s and 1990s. Figures of Luke Skywalker, a character from the 1977 movie *Star Wars*, and G.I. Joe, a popular soldier/adventurer toy, were much more muscular in the 1990s. Mark Hamill, who played Skywalker in the movie *Star Wars*, reportedly said, "They've put me on steroids," when he saw his 1990s action figure.

People who are overweight have been dealing with size bias for a long time, and that bias has never been quiet. Movies such as *Shallow Hal* (2001), in which actress Gwyneth Paltrow wore a fat suit, and *Norbit (2007)*, in which actor Eddie Murphy donned a fat suit, are viewed by some as movie-length fat jokes. In both cases, the movies make fun at the expense of the overweight characters. Story lines involving overweight characters also pop up on television shows. One recurring theme is to have an overweight character cause the death of another character because of his or her weight. In the 1990s, a character on the series *Picket Fences* rolled over in her sleep and suffocated her husband. A similar story line was used on the CBS investigative drama show *CSI.*

In her 2006 article, "Why Fat Jokes Aren't Funny," Barbara D'Souza argued that these plotlines are hurtful, though many of those affected do not speak up. "Since fatness is seen as a lifestyle choice. . . many people tell themselves it's okay to laugh at the overweight." She said that the overweight are just as likely to think about the way they look as temporary. Because they can, in theory, lose the weight, they try to laugh off the jokes. They try to ignore the stares when they go to eat. The fat jokes, however, are not always restricted to the overweight. Now they are being directed at relatively thin people.

Hollywood weights have dropped dramatically since the "golden age" of cinema. Marilyn Monroe, one of the best-known actresses, and in her time considered one of the most beautiful women in Hollywood, wore a size 12 dress. Movie stars now have whittled their weights down to an average size 2 or even 0, and their weight is a constant source of media attention.

In 2007, former Victoria's Secret model Tyra Banks was photographed on vacation in a swimsuit. Since retiring from modeling, the 5-foot 10-inch Banks had gained 30 pounds, putting her at 161 pounds. Magazines, Web sites, and celebrity news TV shows printed the photos and made note of how the model had put on weight. A few days later, Banks appeared on her TV talk show in the same swimsuit. She looked much thinner than the photos in the tabloid, which she felt were taken from an unflattering angle. Banks angrily addressed the photographers and anyone else who looked down on overweight women. She then appeared in a *People* magazine spread in February 2007 wearing a red swimsuit and talked about her experience. She is aware of how negative comments about her can hurt young women. "I get so much mail from young girls who say, 'I look up to you; you're not as skinny as everyone else; I think you're beautiful. So when [the tabloids] say that my body is 'ugly' and 'disgusting,' what does that make those girls feel like?"

Later in 2007, an unflattering photo of actress Jennifer Love Hewitt in a swimsuit appeared in celebrity magazines and on Web sites. Yet, on the Web, along with the photo, people weighed in with their own comments, such as, "She needs to do some jogging. Badly." Hewitt, who says she wears a size 2, struck back on her Web site by writing a letter to the public. "I've sat by in silence for a long time now about the way women's bodies are constantly scrutinized. To set the record straight, I'm not upset for me, but for all of the girls out there that are struggling with their body image. A size two is not fat! Nor will it ever be. And being a size zero doesn't make you beautiful."

STAYING STRONG

Being overweight is one problem that Greg Smith does not have. At 65 pounds, Smith is unable to hold himself upright. He was born with muscular dystrophy (MS). MS is a genetic disease that affects a person's strength. Both bone and muscle strength can be affected. As Smith grew up, many operations were performed to help him combat the disease, including one in which metal rods were implanted in his spine. Even so, Smith is unable to sit upright in his wheelchair without the use of a strap. Yet, this father of three and author of *On a Roll* is undaunted. Smith is a motivational speaker and travels around the world hoping to make a difference in people's lives. Smith uses the media to speak for people with disabilities. His role as a sports commentator and radio host has made him accessible to all kinds of people. *On a Roll* was first a movie about Smith's life. Now the memoir reaches more people. It is mainly about inspiration and how he has used his disability as an asset.

Smith sees every challenge as an opportunity for victory. In one chapter of the book, he describes being home alone and having a pizza and a bottle of soda delivered. When the pizza arrived, he forgot to ask the delivery person to open the soda bottle. After downing a couple of slices,

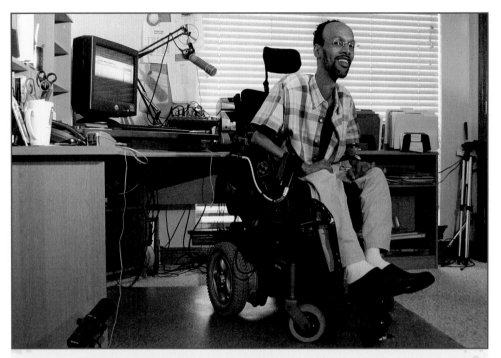

Author, motivational speaker, and radio host Greg Smith works in his home studio where he broadcasts his national radio shows. Smith found inner strength to live a full life and break stereotypes despite having muscular dystrophy.

Smith was thirsty, but the 2-liter bottle was more than he could lift. He considered asking his neighbors for help but was determined to do it on his own. A series of experiments followed, beginning with running the bottle under hot tap water, to creating a lever using duct tape and a drumstick. Finally, Smith went out to the garage to look for some tools. He spotted a dartboard. After stabbing the bottle on both sides with the plastic dart, Smith finally was able to quench his thirst.

This kind of attitude is what has made Smith the success that he is. Raised by a football coach, Smith thinks in terms of victory and defeat. In his life, though he has been dealt

THE SPECIAL OLYMPICS

When most people think about athletes, they think about perfect, well-toned bodies and powerful people. But Eunice Kennedy Shriver decided that those were not the only kind of athletes. In 1962, she invited 35 boys and girls to a summer day camp at her home. All of them had some form of intellectual disability, or mental retardation. The following year, there were 11 such day camps around the United States. By 1968, the Special Olympics had officially begun.

The Olympics is a sporting event that represents the best of the best in every sport from countries all around the world. Shriver wanted everyone to understand that people with disabilities could show their best, too. In 1968, the first Special Olympics hosted 1,000 athletes

(continues)

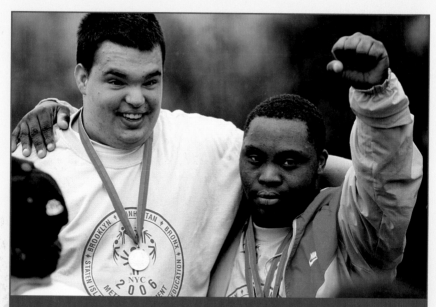

Athletes Jeffrey Dorohow and Danny Fletcher, both of Long Island, New York, receive medals for competing in the shotput competition at the 18th annual Special Olympics Metro Tournament at Riverbank State Park in New York in 2006.

(continued)

from the United States and Canada. On the Special Olympics' Web site, the mayor of Chicago, Richard Daley, reportedly told Eunice Shriver, "The world will never be the same after this."

Today, the Special Olympics sponsors events all over the world. Two-and-a-half million athletes from 165 countries participate in the games to showcase their talent. The 30 Olympic-style summer and winter games show the world that the intellectually disabled are not as incapable as they were once believed to be. Through the efforts of the founders and the use of the media, the image of these people has changed dramatically. Plus, in addition to improved physical ability, the athletes gain better self-esteem and a better self-image.

many things that might have defeated others, Smith says in his book that everyone can "build inner strength by lifting the weights of life's challenges."

LISTENING TO THE DEAF

Some disabilities are harder to spot but equally subject to prejudice. The deaf community has had to fight for equality. For many years, very few deaf children were educated because some felt that education was a waste of time for them. The first schools for the deaf provided an education, but teachers still viewed their deaf students as abnormal. The Rehabilitation Act of 1974 (which was later renamed the Americans with Disabilities Act) put an end to discrimination against disabled workers. It also paved the way for better education for students with disabilities. However, major change did not happen until some disgruntled students decided it was time for different tactics.

Gallaudet University in Washington, D.C., was established in 1864. At the time, it was the only four-year college for deaf and hearing-impaired students. In its long history, the president of the university had always been a hearing person. In 1988 that all changed. The current president was stepping down, and three people were being considered for the position. Two of them were deaf; one was not. When Elisabeth Zinser was appointed as president, the students went into an uproar. Zinser was the non-deaf candidate. They argued that the school was teaching them to be leaders, but they were not willing to put a deaf person in the top leadership position at the school. According to Gallaudet University's archives of these events, the board of trustees chairperson, Jane Spilman, met with students and said, "Deaf people are not able to function in a hearing world."

Finally, both women were replaced. Zinser was replaced with I. King Jordan, the university's first deaf president. Jordan did very well for the school over the next several years. He increased the amount of money that was given to the school from $5 million to $150 million, and more graduates went on to graduate school or to full-time jobs. A 2005 *Washington Post* article reported that students compared Jordan's leadership to that of Dr. Martin Luther King Jr.

BUILDING TOLERANCE

"If you love people, you have no time to judge them."

—*Mother Teresa (1910–1997),*
Catholic nun and missionary

In journalist Malcolm Gladwell's book, *Blink*, one student took the Implicit Association Test (IAT) every day. The race version of the test assessed his preference for white or African-American people. His test results consistently showed that he had a slight preference for whites. On one particular day, he found that his results showed no preference between whites and African-Americans. Normally, there is no way to change your IAT score. Even if you consciously try to think before you answer questions, the score will not change. He could not figure out how his score had changed on that one day. Then he realized that he had been watching the Summer Olympics that morning. There were a lot of black athletes winning medals. He figured out that, because he had recently seen African Americans in a positive light, the association helped to change his score.

If we want to change the way we think about people, we need to look at them in a positive light. The media's portrayals of different groups can be harmful because they do not represent everyone. They also may not give a fair sampling of the group as a whole. The Canadian media has associated immigrants with crimes, but immigrants were found to commit fewer crimes than native-born Canadians. People who see these images and news reports are more likely to think of immigrants and crime as linked. If people were to see positive images of immigrants, that association would likely change, as it did for the student who took the IAT test after watching the Olympics.

Look for images of people of different groups doing positive things. Look around you in your community. Look at your friends and classmates. If there is a group that you would like to know more about that is not in your community, search for books and articles about them. There is plenty of information about people with disabilities who are doing extraordinary things despite their handicaps. There are books and articles about women who have changed the world and about Arab Americans who have done great things for society. Take a trip to the library and seek out information about different groups. Find out who their heroes are. Share their stories with others.

BUILD UNDERSTANDING

Intolerance of others is sometimes about fear. The martial arts expert Bruce Lee once said, "People fear what they do not understand." This may have been true in the case of the Pilgrims who encountered the Native Americans. They did not understand their culture. Eventually they even tried to change it by introducing the Native Americans to a new religion. Red Jacket understood that it was important to hold on to his own culture and the teachings of his ancestors. He also understood that it was important to allow people to hold on to their own culture and beliefs. However, he was not opposed to learning about the culture of the people around him.

One way that people can understand each other's differences is to talk about them. Ask questions in a respectful way. Learn as much as you can, so that you can understand why different groups of people do the things that they do. One group's customs might be very different than your own.

This education is also a way to build relationships. When Rick Givens went on a fact-finding mission to Mexico, he did not know very much about the immigrants who were settling in Siler City, North Carolina. He did know that he wanted them out of the state. His opinion changed once he arrived in Mexico and began to understand their background. When he returned, some people called him a traitor, but Givens had become informed. If everyone had taken the time to find out more about the immigrants they wanted to throw out of their city, they might have changed their minds, too.

THE OASIS OF PEACE

In 1970, an Israeli-born Jew who later became a Catholic priest came to live on the side of a mountain in Israel. He had a vision to build a community of Jews, Arabs, and Christians. He believed that he could fulfill a prophecy from the Old Testaments book of *Isaiah*, which reads, "My people shall dwell in an oasis of peace." A couple of years later, one family joined him. Then many others joined them. Today, the Oasis of Peace lives out the vision of Father Bruno long after his death. Half of the inhabitants are Jewish and the other half are Palestinian Arabs. Their children attend a bilingual and bicultural school. Each classroom has one Jewish and one Arab teacher. In December, the students celebrate Christmas, Eid al-Fitr, and Hanukkah together.

The primary goal of the community is education. These people believe that the way to create a community of equals is by being educated about the people they are in conflict with and by learning to understand them. The School for Peace began in 1979 and has courses for children and adults.

Each family is faithful to its own culture and religion but respects the culture and religion of its neighbors. More than 50 families now live

Find out more about the people in your community who come from different cultures. You might learn that you can help integrate them into American culture, just as Givens decided to help out the schools he visited in Mexico. By making helping the immigrants he met a priority, he found some common ground with people he had once been against.

CELEBRATE

By nature, people separate themselves into different categories. You will belong to many different groups. You might be female, white, and Irish. Explore your own culture. Find out more about where your family is from. Find out more about

together in the community, and many more people want to become a part of the community. Many people outside of the Oasis of Peace send their children to school there. Since the school began, it has served more than 35,000 children. The school is now starting a library that concentrates on Arab/Jewish relations, conflict resolution, and the effect of education on society.

As conflict between Jews and Arabs in Israel continues, the Oasis of Peace hopes that it will be an example for others. Yet, some inhabitants believe that they are "living in a bubble." While the residents shy away from politics, they also believe that they are the only working example of Jews and Palestinians living side-by-side in peace. They all work together for their community. It is difficult to become a new member of the community because people rarely move out.

Although other communities have not embraced the living conditions at the Oasis of Peace, the school has inspired others. Other schools in the area have begun bilingual and bicultural classes based on its model. You can learn more about this community at www.oasisofpeace.org.

the groups to which you belong. Celebrate your own culture and uniqueness.

Some resources for finding out about different groups of people include the Museum of Tolerance (www.museumof-tolerance.com), *Teaching Tolerance* magazine (www.teach-ingtolerance.org), the Anti-Defamation League (www.adl.org), and the National Conference for Community and Justice (www.nccj.org).

Discuss ways that you and other people in your school or community can celebrate their cultural differences. A culture fair, where people can show off their native foods, kinds of dress, dances, and heroes, would be a good way to share the best in each person's culture. The more you find out about people, the less likely you will be to make judgments about them.

COMMUNICATE

In some cultures, it is considered impolite to look someone directly in the eye. In our culture, if someone does not look us in the eye, we might think he or she is trying to hide something. However, if we understand the culture of the person we are talking to, we are less likely to make that kind of judgment. Different cultures have different ways of communicating. The more we understand about those different cultures, the better we will be able to communicate with the people around us.

Once you know a bit more about different cultures, you can help different groups communicate. As a conflict mediator, you can help people find common ground. Once people realize that they are more alike than they are different, they can find understanding.

DO SOMETHING

When Ann Williams stood up for Elizabeth Eckford, she made a lasting impression. She never told Eckford that her family had to get armed guards at their home for supporting integration, but her actions were what Eckford needed. She needed a friend at a time that was very difficult for her. Whenever you can, be a friend to people who are different. It may mean more to them than you realize. Think about what you would feel like if you were in their position. Think of what you could do that would make them feel like they have someone they can trust.

It is important to speak up against prejudiced ideas or language. "You are not only responsible for what you say, but also for what you do not say," Sixteenth century German monk Martin Luther once said. Eckford and the other Little Rock Nine were hoping for support when they walked into their new high school in 1957. Unfortunately, few were willing to give just that.

GET TOGETHER

Dr. Laz found that music, which had helped his special-needs students to communicate, could break barriers for the African-American and Hasidic Jewish teens in Crown Heights, Brooklyn. It helped them to get past their differences and the hate that had boiled over during the riots; it brought them together.

Different clubs might be a way to get diverse groups together. Music, art, poetry, knitting, and dance could be used to integrate groups of different people in a common interest. Even though there are some things that separate people, there are many other things that unite us all.

GLOSSARY

abolition   The ending of slavery

apartheid   An Afrikaans word meaning "apartness"; an official policy of racial segregation followed by the Republic of South Africa until 1994 when all people were allowed to vote in a democratic election.

ban   Prohibit

boycott   To refrain from buying or using products or services

Communism   A system of social organization where property is owned by everyone in common; a system formerly practiced by the Union of Soviet Socialist Republics (U.S.S.R.)

convention   A meeting or formal assembly to discuss a topic of concern

convert   Cause someone to change their religion

councils   Assemblies of persons chosen or elected

delegation   A group chosen to represent a political unit, such as a state or country

desegregate   To eliminate racial segregation

discriminate   To make a judgment against someone because of the group they belong to

enlist   To enroll voluntarily for military service

evacuation   The removal of people from one place to another

integration   To bring together different racial, religious, or ethnic groups

internment camps   Detention centers for political enemies and those with ties to them

missionaries   People sent by a church to spread their religion, teach, or do hospital work

offense   Something that causes anger or displeasure

petition   A written request with the names of the persons making the request

prejudice   Unreasonable negative feelings or opinions about a racial, religious, or ethnic group; when a person forms an opinion before knowing the facts

rally   An event organized for people to come together for a common effort

ratify   To give legal approval for a change

reservation   A place set aside for a specific purpose

resign   To give up a position

resolution   A formal expression of an opinion made after a vote by a group

segregation   The policy or practice of separating people based on their race, class, ability, etc.

stereotype   An oversimplified image or set concept of a group of people

supremacy   The highest or greatest rank or quality

tarnished   Spoiled

tenure   Time period for holding an office or position

tolerance   A fair and objective attitude toward people of different races, religions, abilities, customs, or nationalities

BIBLIOGRAPHY

Aaseng, Nathan. *Navajo Code Talkers*. New York: Walker and Company, 1994.

Adler, David A. *A Picture Book of Jackie Robinson*. New York: Holiday House, 1994.

"The Bad Old Days Are Here Again: At Gallaudet University, It's 1968 All over Again." *Weekly Standard*, October 23, 2006.

Bolden, Tonya. *Portraits of African-American Heroes*. New York: Penguin Young Readers Group, 2005.

Carter, Bob. "Ashe's Impact Reached Far Beyond Court." *ESPN Sportscentury Biography*, 2007.

Chappell, Kevin. "Nation Reflects on Legacy of Little Rock." *Jet*, October 15, 2007.

Eagle, Lynne. "Media Literacy as an Educational Method for Addressing College Women's Body Image Issues." *Education*, Summer 2007.

"The Economics of Ethnic and Racial Stereotyping." Media Awareness Network. Available online. URL: http://www.media-awareness.ca/english/issues/stereotyping/ethnics_and_minorities_economics.cfm. Accessed January 17, 2008.

"Ethnic and Visible Minorities in Entertainment Media." Media Awareness Network. Available online. URL: http://www.media-awareness.ca/english/issues/stereotyping/ethnics_and_minorities_economics.cfm. Accessed January 17, 2008.

Franey, Lynn. "Lesson of Tenacity over Racial Taunts." *Kansas City Star*, June 22, 2007.

Golenbock, Peter. *Teammates*. New York: Harcourt Children's Books, 1992.

Guzman, Lila, and Rick Guzman. *Cesar Chavez Fighting for Fairness*. Berkeley Heights, N.J.: Enslow Publishers, 2006.

Kifner, John, and Felicia R. Lee. "In Crown Heights, a Decade of Healing After Riots, but Scars Remain." *New York Times*, August 19, 2001.

Kirk, John A. "Crisis at Central High." *History Today*, September 2007. Available online. URL: http://www.historytoday.com. Accessed November 11, 2007.

"Piling on the Prejudice." BBC News Online Magazine, September 6, 2004. Available online. URL: http://news.bbc.co.uk/2/hi/uk_news/magazine/3622320.stm. Accessed January 10, 2008.

Rappoport, Ken. *Profiles in Sports Courage*. New York: Peachtree Publishers, 2006.

"Red Jacket and the Decolonization of Republican Virtue." *American Indian Quarterly*, Fall 2007.

"Red Jacket Defends Native American Religion, 1805." History Matters. Available online. URL: http://historymatters.gmu.edu/d/5790. Accessed January 13, 2008.

Robinson, Sharon. *Promises to Keep: How Jackie Robinson Changed America*. New York: Scholastic, 2004.

Rodriguez, Consuelo. *Cesar Chavez*. New York: Chelsea House Publishers, 2001.

Schomp, Virginia. *American Voices from the Women's Movement*. New York: Marshall Cavendish Benchmark, 2007.

"Spady A. Koyama Overcame Bias as a 'Yankee Samurai.'" *Star-Ledger*, March 24, 2006.

"Tools of Exclusion: Race, Disability, and (Re)segregated Education." 2005. Available online. URL: http://www.digitaldivide.net/comm/docs/view.php?DocID=312. Accessed January 18, 2008.

"WGA Diversity Report Has 'Familiar Ring to It.'" *Hollywood Reporter*. May 8, 2007. Available online. URL: http://www.sag.org/node/343. Accessed March 11, 2008.

Winerip, Michael. "Learning-Disabled Students Blossom in Blended Classes." *New York Times*, November 30, 2005.

Wright, Pamela Darr, and Peter W.D. Wright. *From Emotions to Advocacy: The Special Education Survival Guide.* Hatfield, Va.: Harbor House Law Press, 2001.

Wright, Peter W.D., and Pamela Darr Wright. *Wrightslaw: Special Education Law.* Hatfield, Va.: Harbor House Law Press, 1999.

FURTHER RESOURCES

BOOKS

Counts, Will. *A Life Is More than a Moment*. Bloomington: Indiana University Press, 1999.

Davis, Barbara J. *The National Grape Boycott*. Mankato, Minn.: Compass Point Books, 2008.

Frank, Anne. *Diary of a Young Girl*. New York: Bantam Books, 1993.

Gladwell, Malcolm. *Blink*. New York: Little, Brown, 2005.

Haley, Alex. *Roots*. New York: Vanguard Press, 2007.

Hughes, Langston. *Thank You, Ma'am*. New York: The Creative Company, 1993.

Nolte, Dorothy Law, and Rachel Harris. *Children Learn What They Live*. New York: Workman Publishing Company, 1998.

Oughton, Jerrie. *Music from a Place Called Half Moon*. New York: Houghton Mifflin, 1995.

Steinbeck, John. *The Grapes of Wrath*. New York: Penguin Putnam, 2002.

Taylor, Mildred D. *Let the Circle Be Unbroken*. New York: Penguin Young Readers Group, 2002.

WEB SITES

Teaching Tolerance Magazine
www.teachingtolerance.org
The site includes information for students about fighting hate.

The Anti-Defamation League
www.adl.org
The league and its site are dedicated to fighting anti-Semitism, racism, and extremism.

Facing History and Ourselves

www.facing.org

The organization and its site are dedicated to helping students become more humane citizens.

Museum of Tolerance

www.museumoftolerance.org

The site provides education, information about exhibits, and resources on human rights issues.

National Conference for Community and Justice

www.nccj.org

The organization and its site are dedicated to fighting bias, bigotry, and racism.

National Council of La Raza

www.nclr.org

This Latino civil rights and advocacy organization offers resources for those fighting for civil rights.

Harvard University's Implicit Association

https://implicit.harvard.edu/implicit/

This is a test research site.

PICTURE CREDITS

Page:

17: Zuma/Newscom

19: Courtesy of Dr. Laz

23: The Granger Collection

27: AP Images

30: Courtesy of David Koyama

33: Sipa/Newscom

35: Courtesy of David Koyama

36: AP Images

41: AP Images

42: The Granger Collection

44: Sipa/Newscom

47: MRP/Newscom

54: Getty Hulton/Newscom

56: Bettmann/Corbis

59: AP Images

70: Picturehistory/ Newscom

72: Picturehistory/ Newscom

75: Getty Hulton/Newscom

77: Getty Hulton/Newscom

79: Sipa/Newscom

81: AP Images

87: AP Images

102: Joanne Caputo Films

103: AP Images

INDEX

A

Aaron, Hank, 48
ableism, 63
action figures, 99
advertising, 97–98
Afghanistan, 79–80
AFL-CIO. *See* American
  Federation of Labor and
  Congress of Industrial
  Organizations
African Americans
  baseball and, 39–51
  education and, 52–61
  image of in media, 96–97
  nooses and, 17, 20
  voting rights and, 73, 76
age, Implicit Association Test
  and, 15
Agricultural Workers
  Organizing Committee
  (AWOC), 86
Alexander, Susan, 98
Allied Translator and
  Interpreter Section, 32
American Federation of Labor
  and Congress of Industrial
  Organizations (AFL-CIO),
  86, 88
American Woman Suffrage
  Association, 76
Americans with Disabilities
  Act, 104
Amin, Qasim, 68
anabolic steroids, 98–99
Anson, Cap, 40
Anti-Defamation League, 110
Anti-Slavery Convention, 69–71
apartheid, 46–47
Aristotle, 10
Aryans, 47–48
Ashe, Arthur, 46–47
AWOC. *See* Agricultural
  Workers Organizing
  Committee

B

Bandaranaike, Sirimavo, 74
Banks, Tyra, 100
baseball
  beginnings of, 39–41
  integration and, 43–45
  Jackie Robinson and,
    43–51
  segregated teams and,
    41–43
Basque Redondo, 26
Bates, Daisy, 55, 57
Black Image in the White Mind
  (Entman and Rojecki), 97
Blink (Gladwell), 14–15, 106
Board of Education, Brown v.,
  53, 63
Boone, Herman, 50
border security, 93–94
Borlaug, Norman, 11
Britain, 69
Brodie, Ralph, 59
Brooklyn Brown Dodgers, 43
Brooks, Crystal, 60
Brown, Oliver L., 53
Brown v. Board of Education,
  53, 63
Bush, George W., 28–29, 34

C

Camp Florida Fishtales, 66
Campanella, Roy, 43
Cartwright, Alexander Joy,
  39–41
Cato, Gavin, 18
Center for New North
  Carolinians, 92
Central High School, 55–61, 111
cerebral palsy, 64
Chambers, Karen, 98
Chandler, Paul, 18–19
Chapman, Ben, 49–50
character deficit, 8
character education, 9–10

Character Matters (Lickona), 9
Chavez, Cesar, 83–89
Chicago White Stockings, 40
Children Now study, 96
China, 69
Civil War, 73
Clinton, William J., 38
coaching, integration and, 50
code talkers, 25–29
Cohen, Jeff, 97
collaborative team teaching, 67
Columbine High School, 16
Comanche people, 26
Community Service Organization (CSO), 86
Congressional Gold Medal, 11
Congressional Medal of Honor, 9, 26, 38
Counts, Will, 55–56, 60
Crow, Jim, 39
CSO. *See* Community Service Organization
Cuadros, Paul, 90–91
Cuomo, Mario, 19
CURE project, 18–19

D
Daley, Richard, 104
Dawson's Creek, 97
deafness, 104–105
Debrauwere, Lauren, 7
Declaration of Sentiments, 71
Delano grape farms, 88–89
disabilities, people with, 15, 18–19, 61–67, 101–105
Douglass, Frederick, 73
D'Souza, Barbara, 100
Dubester, Ilana, 93
Duke, David, 90–91
Dunham, Jason, 8–9

E
Eckford, Elizabeth, 55–57, 60–61, 110–111
Educating for Character (Lickona), 9

education
culture and, 108–109
deafness and, 104–105
disabled and, 61–67, 104–105
immigrants and, 89
integration of Central High School and, 55–61
lawsuits and, 53–57
migrant workers and, 84, 85
segregation and, 52, 55–61
understanding and, 107–108
women and, 68–69, 71, 73, 78–81
Education for All Handicapped Children Act (EHA), 62–63
Egypt, 68
EHA. *See* Education for All Handicapped Children Act
Einwag, Brian, 66
Eisenhower, Dwight D., 53, 57
Eisenhower, Fabus v., 53–57
Entman, Robert, 97
Equal Pay Act, 78, 81
Equal Rights Amendment, 78
Eshkol, Levi, 74
ethics, study on students and, 8
Executive Order 9066, 30–38

F
Fabus v. Eisenhower, 53–57
Fairness and Accuracy in Media, 97
Faubus, Orval, 53, 57
Felicity, 97
Ferguson, Plessy v., 52
Fifteenth Amendment, 73, 76
Florida Fishtales Camp, 66
foot-binding, 69
Foster, Jaime, 92
Fourteenth Amendment, 73
"Fulfilling the Dream" Award, 19

G
Gallaudet University, 104–105
Gandhi, Indira Priyadarshini, 74

Gandhi, Mohandas "Mahatma," 84–85
Gates, Bill, 11
gender roles, 15. *See also* Women's rights
Getting Even: Why Women Don't Get Paid Like Men and What to Do About It (Murphy), 81–82
Gibson, Josh, 48
Gitchell, Dent, 58
Givens, Rick, 91–93, 108–109
Giver, The (Lowry), 13
Gladwell, Malcolm, 14–15, 106
grandfather clause, 76
grape farming, 88–89
Green, Ernest, 57–58
Green Revolution, 11

H
Hamill, Mark, 99
Harris, Eric, 16
Hasidic Jews, 18–19, 111
Hewitt, Jennifer Love, 101
Hitler, Adolf, 16–17, 47–48
home values, 90

I
IDEA. *See* Individuals with Disabilities Education Act
image
    deafness and, 104–105
    media and, 95–96, 101, 106–107
    people with disabilities and, 101–105
    size-bias and, 98–101
    video games and, 96–98
immigrants
    complaints about, 89–91
    image and, 107
    migrant workers and, 83–89
    North Carolina and, 89–91, 92–94, 108
Implicit Association Test, 15, 106
inclusion, defined, 63
"Increase the Peace" slogan, 18–19

India, 74, 84–85
Individuals with Disabilities Education Act (IDEA), 62–65
Inouye, Daniel, 33–34
integration, 43–45, 50, 54–55. *See also* education; segregation
internment camps, 31–32, 34
Iraq, 8–9
Iroquois people, 22
Israel, 74, 108–109
Isum, Rachel, 48

J
Jamie Foxx Show, The, 97
Japanese Americans, World War II and, 30–38
Jena High School, 17, 20
Jim Crow Laws, 39, 42, 48
John Lindsay Award, 19
Johnston, Phillip, 26
Jordan, I. King, 105
Jordan-Matthews High School, 90–91
Josephson Institute of Ethics, 8

K
Kilpatrick, William, 7–8
Klebold, Dylan, 16
Koyama, Spady, 30–38
Ku Klux Klan (KKK), 90–91

L
labor organizations, 86, 88–89
language, education system and, 89–90
Lapchick, Richard, 46–47
Lazerson, David, 18–19, 111
Lee, Bruce, 107
Lickona, Thomas, 9
Lindsay Award, 19
Ludden, Jennifer, 91–92
Luther, Martin, 111

M
MacPhail, Larry, 43
Man Whose Arms Exploded, The, 99
Marshall, Thurgood, 53

mass media, 95–96
Massery, Hazel Bryan, 56–57, 60
Mays, Willie, 48
McDonnell (Father), 84–85
McEnroe, John, 47
McHughes, Josh, 58–59
Medal of Honor, 9, 26, 38
media, 95–96, 99–101, 106–107
Meir, Golda, 74
Melican, Debra Burns, 97
Mexican Americans, 83–89
migrant workers, 83–89
Military Intelligence Service
    Language School, 32
Miller, James, 24
Monroe, James, 24
Monroe, Marilyn, 100
Montreal Royals, 45, 48–49
Moore, Angela, 60
moral illiteracy, 7–8
Mother Hale Award, 19
Mother Teresa, 11
Mothershed-Wair, Thelma, 58
motivational speaking, 101
Mott, Lucretia, 69–73
Mullane, Tony, 40
Munoz, Irma, 97
Murphy, Eddie, 99
Murphy, Evelyn F., 81–82
muscular dystrophy, 101
Museum of Tolerance, 110
Muslims, 34

N
NAACP, 53, 54, 55
National Character Counts
    Week, 8
National Conference for
    Community and Justice, 110
National Farm Workers
    Association (NFWA), 86–87
National Guard, 55, 57
National Woman Suffrage
    Association, 73, 76
National Woman's Party, 77
Native Americans
        Navajo code talkers and,
        25–29
        Pilgrims and, 21–22, 107

preserving culture of,
    24–25
    Red Jacket and, 22–24,
    107
Navajo code talkers, 25–29
Navajo War, 26
Negro Leagues, 41–43, 48
New York Foundation Peace
    Award, 19
New York Knickerbockers
    (baseball), 41
Newcombe, Don, 43
news reports, 96
NFWA. *See* National Farm
    Workers Association
Nicomachean Ethics (Aristotle),
    10
Nobel Peace Prize, 11
nooses, 17, 20
Norbit, 99
North Carolina, 89–91, 92–94
North Carolina and, 108–109
Northern Illinois University
    shooting, 7

O
Oasis of Peace, 108–109
Ogden Council, 24
Ogden Land Company, 24
Olympics, 46, 103–104, 106–107
On a Roll (Smith), 101

P
Paige, Satchel, 48
Palestine, 108–109
Paltrow, Gwyneth, 99
Pankhurst, Emmeline and
    Christabel, 69, 76
Parmenter, Dan, 7
Pattillo-Beals, Melba, 58
Paul, Alice, 76–78
Picket Fences, 99
Pilgrims, 21–22, 107
Pinker, Steven, 10–11
Plessy v. Ferguson, 52
poll taxes, 76
poultry farms, 89
Presidential Medal of Freedom,
    11

Profiles in Sports Courage
(Rappoport), 44
profiling, 14
P.S. 75, 66–67
Purple Hearts, 37

Q
Quakers, 69–71, 76

R
race, 15, 18–19. *See also* African
Americans
rapid cognition, 14–15
Rappoport, Ken, 44
Red Jacket, 22–25, 107
Reese, Pee Wee, 49, 51
Rehabilitation Act of 1974, 104
Reinhardt, Ken, 61
religion, 15, 22–24
Remember the Titans, 50
Revolutionary War, 22
Rickey, Branch, 43–44, 48–49
Robinson, Jackie, 43–51
Robinson, Jerry, 45
Robinson, Mack, 45–48
Robinson, Mallie, 45
Robison, Lynne, 63–66
Rojecki, Andrew, 97
On a Roll (Smith), 101
Roosevelt, Franklin D., 34
rounders, 39

S
Sagoyewatha (Red Jacket),
22–25, 107
Sal Si Puedes, 84–85
Sarabi, Habiba, 79–80
segregation, 39–52, 55–61, 63.
See also Integration
self-image, size-bias and, 98–99
Seneca people, 22. *See also* Red
Jacket
September 11 attacks, 33
Shallow Hal, 99
sharecropping, 45
Shastri, Lal Bahadur, 74
Shriver, Eunice Kennedy, 103–
104

size-bias, image and, 98–101
skin color, Implicit Association
Test and, 15
Skullcaps 'n' Switchblades
(Lazerson), 18
Skywalker, Luke, 99
Smith, Albert, 29
Smith, Greg, 101–104
soccer, 80, 90–91
Soldiers National Cemetery, 50
South Africa, 46–47
special education, 61–67
Special Olympics, 103–104
Spilman, Jane, 105
Sri Lanka, 74
Stanton, Elizabeth Cady, 71–73,
76
steroids, 98–99
Steve Harvey Show, The, 97
Stovall, Jim, 10
strikes, 88–89
suffragettes, 69, 76–78
swastikas, 16–17
symbols, power of, 16–17, 20

T
Takao Ozawa v. U.S., 31–32
Taliban, 80
taxes, 69, 76, 90, 93
Teaching Tolerance magazine,
110
television, 95–97, 99
tennis, 46–47
Teresa (Mother), 11
terrorism, 33
Thanksgiving, 21–22
Thatcher, Margaret, 74
Third Reich, 16–17
Thomas, Jefferson, 58
Title IX, 78
Toledo Blue Stockings, 40
town ball, 40
Trickey, Minnijean Brown, 58
Truth, Sojourner, 76

U
Ultimate Gift, The (Stovall), 10
Ungerleider, Charles, 96

unions, 86–87, 88–89
U.S., Takao Ozawa v., 31–32

V
video games, 96–98
Vinson, Fred M., 53
voter qualification laws, 76
Votes for Women newsletter, 69
voting rights
    Mexican Americans and,
      85–86
    taxes and, 69, 76
    women and, 71–73, 76–78

W
WAGE Project, 81–82
Walker, Moses Fleetwood, 40
War of 1812, 24
Warren, Earl, 53
Washington, Denzel, 50
Washington, George, 22
weight, 15, 98–101
wheelchairs, 101

*Why Can't Johnny Tell Right from
    Wrong?* (Kilpatrick), 7–8
Williams, Ann, 61, 110–111
Wilson, Nancy, 60
Wilson, Woodrow, 78
WNBA, 80
women's rights
    education and, 68–69, 71,
      73, 78–81
    history of, 68–73
    sports and, 78, 80
    voting rights and, 71–73,
      76
Women's Rights Convention,
    71–73
World War II, 25–29, 30–38

Y
Yankee Samurai, 32–38
Yoast, Bill, 50

Z
Zinser, Elizabeth, 105

ABOUT THE AUTHOR AND CONSULTANTS

Tracey Baptiste is the author of the young-adult novel *Angel's Grace*, which was named one of the 100 Best Books for Reading and Sharing in 2005 by New York City public librarians. She has also written biographies of *Jerry Spinelli* and *Madeleine L'Engle*, both in Chelsea House's WHO WROTE THAT? series, as well as another title in Character Education, *Being a Leader and Making Decisions*. Find out more about Baptiste at www.traceybaptiste.com.

Series consultant **Dr. Madonna Murphy** is a professor of education at the University of St. Francis in Joliet, Illinois, where she teaches education and character education courses to teachers. She is the author of *Character Education in America's Blue Ribbon Schools* and *History & Philosophy of Education: Voices of Educational Pioneers*. She has served as the character education consultant for a series of more than 40 character education books for elementary school children, on the Character Education Partnership's Blue Ribbon Award committee recognizing K-12 schools for their character education, and on a national committee for promoting character education in teacher education institutions.

Series consultant **Sharon L. Banas** was a middle school teacher in Amherst and Tonawanda, New York, for more than 30 years. She led the Sweet Home Central School District in the development of its nationally acclaimed character education program. In 1992, Sharon was a member of the Aspen Conference, drafting the Aspen Declaration that was approved by the U.S. Congress. In 2001, she published *Caring Messages for a School Year*. She has been married to her husband, Doug, for 37 years. They have a daughter, son, and new granddaughter.